SKYWALKER

HIGHS AND LOWS
ON THE PACIFIC CREST TRAIL

By Bill Walker

Dedication

My mother, Kathleen Malloy Walker, who has
never given in to the surely strong temptation to
crane her neck up at me and cry out in horror,
"What hath I wrought?"

Disclaimer

This book describes the author's experiences while walking the Pacific Crest Trail and reflects his opinions relating to those experiences. Others may recall these same events differently. Some names and identifying details mentioned in the book have been changed to protect their privacy.

Canada

Mexico

Chapter 1

Worst Lost Ever

The most beautiful adventures are not those we go to seek.

Robert Louis Stevenson

"Is this the worst you've ever been lost hiking?" Lauren suddenly asked me.

It was the afternoon of July 3, 2009. All across America people were heading off in packed cars to barbecues, beaches, and sunny vacations to celebrate the upcoming Independence Day holiday. Lauren and I, however, were confronted with a stunningly contrarian scene. All we could see, for miles on end, was a heavy blanket of snow interspersed with frozen mountain lakes. The last few miles had been up to our waists at times.

Lauren was seventeen years old, and we were hiking together completely by accident. Her mother had heard from a co-worker that his son was planning a hike on the Pacific Crest Trail. Because Lauren had shown some nascent interest in hiking, her mother had inquired— perhaps against her better judgment—about the possibility of Lauren joining her co-worker's son. That had led directly to this mess.

Weeks earlier Lauren had joined up with this proposed hiking partner. His name was Pat, and he was a 26-year old male of extraordinary athletic ability. The two of them had set out together on the hardest part of the Pacific Crest Trail (PCT). It is called the *High Sierra* and reaches the very highest points on the American mainland. By everyone's appraisal, Lauren and Pat were making a game effort.

Having a hiking partner allowed them to share several items, including a tent. This critically reduced their backpack weight. However, because they slept in the same tent, there had been some murmurings on the trail grapevine about Pat trysting with the 17-year old Lauren. But I had seen them up close for several days and nights running, and it seemed all business. All about miles.

A hiking partner also reduces one's chances of getting lost. Theoretically. But Pat was perhaps the fastest hiker I had ever seen, despite having a backpack that looked like it was loaded down with sandbags. He appeared so rhapsodic about hiking in this magnificent mountain setting that I had begun to think he was afflicted with the *Icarus complex*. Pat habitually blasted off ahead of Lauren first thing in the morning. She repeatedly sacrificed breaks, hiking for hours-at-a-time, (earning her the trail name, *No Break*) to keep up with him. One could objectively say she was being courageous.

At the end of the day, when Pat and Lauren were finally reunited at some distant campsite, he often had a slightly embarrassed look on his face—like he couldn't help himself. Maybe he couldn't. Like so many mortals who had preceded him over the eons, he was utterly in the thrall of the High Sierra.

***

Long-distance hiking is inherently conducive to mood swings. But on this 3d day of July, my morale was especially fragile. The previous night I had camped alone, about a half-mile ahead of Pat and Lauren. I had gotten up this morning at first light prepared to clear Muir Pass, the last really difficult, snowy pass in the *High Sierra*. For days I had been anxiously debriefing southbounders passing in the opposite direction about what exactly lay ahead. One after another had reported that the Pass was covered with a thick blanket of snow for miles on each side of the summit.

Not surprisingly, soon after I began trooping this morning, Pat had come jackrabbiting past me.

"Wait for Lauren and me," I yelled ahead to him playfully.

"Yeah, yeah," he said self-consciously. "I'll, uh, see you up at the top."

Yeah, sure!

The biggest problem was simply figuring out where to go. The vast amounts of snowmelt had created more surging streams than I could have ever fathomed. This morning I had been able to follow Pat's footprints through the snow along the western edge of a couple of alpine lakes. But as the PCT started up the face of Muir Pass, the placid lakes and footprints gave way to the heavy rush of water crashing down a ravine. I saw footprints on the far side, which meant I needed to somehow get across.

Tentatively, I edged down the icy bank to get to a large rock. But my feet came out from under me, and I did a base-runner's slide right into the icy running water. I frantically thrashed around attempting to reach the next icy boulder. I didn't completely careen over, but splashed wildly the last several feet in the rushing current getting to the far side. *At least I'm over.*

When I looked back down the hill I spotted Lauren, scoping around trying to decide on a route. Instinctively, I started waving her to come up my way. Lauren dutifully followed my footprints up the left bank, and soon stood at the precipice of the tumbling rapids.

"Here, here," I kept shouting. She looked dubious. For good reason. The spot I was pointing out was shallower, but the current even stronger.

"Right there, there," I kept shouting over at her. "That rock." Finally, we gave up any cross-stream communication, as she hung in suspense atop a jagged boulder, plotting her next step. Water roared by her on all sides, and she took on plenty of it. But soon enough she, too, was across.

"Good goin'," I tried encouraging her. "We'll stick together until we catch up with Pat."

"Alright."

***

When her mother had arranged a hiking partner for her, it was probably just this type of situation she had in mind. But in this case it was just as necessary for *me*. For starters, we were in one of the most isolated areas in the entire United States. Any kind of civilization was days away in any direction. The biggest problem, though, was that due to a post office glitch I didn't have any maps.

"Could I take a quick look at your maps?" I asked Lauren.

"Pat borrowed them last night," she said. *She doesn't have any maps either.* We exchanged worried glances.

"Well, this must be Helen Lake," I motioned at yet another gorgeous, but frozen, alpine lake. "My data book here says it's only a half-mile from the summit." "Good," she said, sounding relieved. But after another half-mile of humping through the snow, lo and behold, another open expanse of frozen water appeared. The silence was pregnant.

"I guess this here is Helen Lake," I finally said in resignation.

Beautiful alpine setting. Hard to believe it is July.

"Well, at least we know we've only got a half-mile to the top," she said matter-of-factly.

"As long as we don't get lost."

Of course, that was just a fallacy. We had been effectively lost for several miles. Sure, we were following Pat's footprints. But Pat was obviously improvising, himself, given that the PCT was completely invisible under the snow. Finally, we followed Pat's footprints up to a steep precipice that led off a cliff. I stepped back and looked at Lauren in disbelief. But not because of the steep dropoff.

"I don't believe it."

"What?" she wondered in wide-eyed fashion.

"Helen Lake," I mourned.

"Gosh, I don't know," she said, temporarily flushed. But quickly she led us down the precipice to better treading.

"Oh, there they are," she said in work-womanlike fashion, when she spotted more footprints. The grades became steeper, which was further confirmation that we were well off the PCT. Then we came to a steep ravine bisected by a rushing creek.

"Look at those footprints up on that icy ledge," I said in amazement. "Those look like Pat's footprints," Lauren said.

"Man, he could have bought it right there," I said with a sense of dread stirring.

I quickly dropped my backpack and ran off to look for another route. But nothing revealed itself.

"Anything?" Lauren asked, when I got back.

"Nope."

"What if we cross that creek down there," she suggested.

"Then what?"

"Well, let's just see."

We scurried down to our right, where rock-hopping across the stream proved to be easy. Soon, we were laboring heavily in a snow field heading straight up the face of Muir Pass. Good breaks are rare this deep in the mountains. But we got one, when we came upon a modest-sized stone hut at the top of Muir Pass.

"Hey, did you know there was a hut?" I yelled back excitedly to Lauren.

"No," she answered.

"Forty-nine percent chance Pat is waiting in there," I ventured. Fat chance.

***

Lauren and I sat there feasting on mediocre hiker fare within the friendly confines of Muir Hut. Suddenly, she blurted out, "This might not be the summit."

"Why would they build the hut here then?" I quickly countered.

"But look ahead," she pointed straight north up the PCT. "Those mountains out there look like they might be higher than where we are here." *This might not be the summit. My God.*

Silence reigned. *If this isn't the summit it might take hours to get to the real summit. We've already been told there is heavy snow for at least the next three miles. There may not be enough time to get down today.* My disaster-prevention instincts were now on high alert. It was time to broach a delicate topic.

"Maybe, the safest thing would be to just stay right here for the night," I said gingerly. Silence.

"I don't know," Lauren finally said in downcast fashion. This young girl was a hiker, not a pretender.

I didn't fancy staying here above 10,000 feet in a damp hut either. I knew the way my long, thin physique would react— shivering and miserable. My heart was for getting out of here. But my head said something different. If we headed out, we were going to be exposed for hours and our chances of getting completely lost were prominent. One regularly hears reports of hikers getting stranded in snowy mountains, followed by search and rescue operations that arrive too late.

Awkward silence. I sensed another subtle factor. How many times had I had witnessed male hikers practically prostrating themselves as they found novel ways to hang around female hikers. Usually it was harmless, and at times actually seemed synergistic. But Lauren was attractive enough, and the breach in ages yawning enough, that my conservative instincts dictated extreme caution, especially in a setting this remote, even intimate.

"I'd rather try going, if it's okay," she said tentatively. One of the great things about long-distance hiking is the way sociology gets turned completely on its head. Many times I had taken my cue from much younger people, and it didn't bother me a wit.

"Alright," I finally said. "But, honestly, if it looks really bad the first mile, I'm just gonna' head back to this hut for the night."

"Okay."

***

The blanket of snow was thicker than anything I'd seen in twenty years. Every so often I'd fall through the crust of ice and straight down a shaft of snow reaching my upper thighs. This is known as *postholing*. Lauren fell behind me as she occasionally postholed all the way up to her waist.

Fortunately, we were easily able to follow Pat's footprints. Down in the valley, Sapphire and Heron Lakes shone brilliantly in the afternoon sunshine. My mood began to lighten and I was glad we had gone.

But then we reached a dogleg in the route we were following. Streams from the snowmelt led wildly through the cavernous valley in all manner of directions. Pat's footprints weren't anywhere to be found. A pattern quickly developed.

"Those look like footprints over there," our navigator, Lauren, would say. I'd drop my backpack and go ricocheting through streams or rushing water to locate footprints on a ridge, only to have them give way to another stream. It was quite tiring, and even more maddening.

Despite the failure of these reconnaissance efforts, we now needed to make the crucial decision. *Had we summited Muir Pass at the hut and, thus, should follow the valley east down towards the lakes? Or was the summit of Muir Pass these steep peaks lying straight in front of us?*

We didn't see footprints on either. More ominously, both routes appeared to disappear into a forbidding, Arctic-like wild. If we chose the wrong one we were likely stranded, at least for the rest of the day, if not much longer.

"What's your gut tell you, Lauren?" I asked. "Up these

mountains straight ahead or down to the right in the valley?"

"I don't know," she said. "I can't believe they didn't put any signs or cairns to give you some idea where to go." Valid point, to be sure. But I was worried about only one thing—how to safely get the hell out of here.

"What about that bank of snow over there?" she wondered. "Weren't there some footprints on that side before." But my adrenaline-fed sloshing around streams was beginning to flag.

"Let's go scout out that side together," I suggested.

"I don't want to fall in the river," she plainly said.

"Where?" I asked.

"There's a river under this snow."

This conjured up a horror story making rounds in the hiker community. A solitary hiker in the High Sierra had decided to camp on a field of snow. Unfortunately, and completely unbeknownst to him, a waterway lay beneath the snow. During the night, his weight and body heat combined to submerge his sleeping-bag enveloped body in the water. He had drowned trapped in his sleeping bag.

***

I was bent over catching my breath. Lauren had all but lost her eagle eye for footprints. Stasis had set in. This is when Lauren blurted out her question ("Is this the worst you've ever been lost hiking?").

She sounded uncharacteristically forlorn. The greater part of valor would have been to give a working response that referred to various options, fallback plans, etc. If ever there was a time for a *Jesuitical lie*, this was it.

Unfortunately, my gut—or perhaps cowardly—instincts reacted decisively. "Never even been close to this lost," I quickly answered.

Chapter 2

Why Long-Distance Hiking?

"Our nature lies in movement. Complete calm is death."

Pascal's Pensees

If the world has a future, it has an ascetic future.

Bruce Chatwin

Wandering is very human. We are essentially nomadic organisms and peaceful by nature. So postulated Britain's notorious travel writer, Bruce Chatwin, in his epic tome, *The Songlines*.

Chatwin had closely followed the migratory patterns of Australia's aboriginal people. Specifically, he noted that they maintained peace with other tribes by singing different verses depending on what natural landscape they encountered. As long as all the tribes kept walking and kept singing, harmony was maintained. However, "civilization took a wrong turn," he nostalgically concluded, "and chose the inferior option." Instead of nomadic wandering, humans have strived to adopt sedentary lifestyles.

Chatwin, himself, was a rather mercurial character. *The Guardian* noted he had "a horror of houses, possessions, fixed abodes", and believed that settlement is "degenerative for humankind." Dead of AIDS at age 49, Chatwin, nonetheless, remains in respectable company regarding his deeply-held belief in the power of continual movement.

The Bedouins, the Moors, the Kurds, and the Indians all felt that to be true to oneself, *perpetual motion* was necessary. History's great religious figures maintained this faith as well. Moses, Jesus, and Mohammed all undertook widespread peregrinations at great peril.

"I know of no thought so burdensome that one can't walk away from it," the Danish theologian, Soren Kierkegaard wrote. "The more one sits still, the closer one comes to feeling ill." The great Russian novelist, Dostoyevsky, maintained that all our miseries stemmed from a single cause—our inability to remain quietly in a room.

Could it be that this distraction—our mania for the new— was in essence an instinctive migratory urge? Darwin, in *The Descent of Man*, noted that in birds the migratory instinct appears overwhelmingly powerful—even stronger than the maternal instinct. A mother will abandon her fledglings in nest rather than miss the long journey south.

***

I, too, have found great fulfillment in being footloose over the years. Looking back, my fondest memories (if not the most exalted actions!) as a kid are of those times together with friends on foot. But once everyone got cars, we steadily grew away from each other.

I've lived in almost a dozen-and-a-half cities over the years, and there is a clear pattern. I've been happiest in those places (Chicago, London, Latin America) where I didn't have and didn't need a car. Like most everybody else I just walked.

In England, I had been surprised to learn that many of the best golf courses didn't even have golf carts.

"What if somebody can't walk?" I once asked my playing partner, a sixtyish Englishman of dour visage.

"Then you don't play," he responded plainly. But to everyone's pleasant surprise, we all found that the level of fulfillment and bonding was much greater when we covered the course on foot. However, when I returned to the United States after 4 ½ years I quickly became disillusioned when I couldn't find anybody to play with who didn't demand a golf cart. It was especially confounding to see people who exercise religiously in gymnasiums, clinging to these *metallic wombs* on the golf course.

This is when I became interested in hiking. In 2005 I attempted a thru-hike of the 2,175 mile Appalachian Trail. Like most people who hike the Appalachian Trail, I was so buoyant upon completion that I found it practically impossible to quit talking about it.

"Why don't you write a book about it?" a few people finally suggested. What they were really hoping for, of course, was to get me to shut up about the whole thing. My big question was whether I could write enough for a whole book. However, the problem ended up being just the opposite. I remembered every one of the 171 days so vividly that I had to agonize over how to cut the book manuscript down to manageable size.

That illustrates a basic phenomenon of long-distance hiking. It is an utterly rich experience. In *The Cactus Eaters*, Dan White described it this way: "Though the trail narrows your choices—hike, sweat, piss, seek water, shit, eat, repeat—somehow it makes your life more expansive." It seemed like a great bargain. You got perhaps two years of living for every six months you were out there. There had been no other such sustained experience for me where life had thrummed at such a high pitch.

After the Appalachian Trail, I went back to work for a private company. However, it quickly became apparent I had a different outlook. Deep in my marrow, I now felt that I could get by just fine with less sleep, less utilities, fewer restaurants, less housing, less insurance, less medicine, less money. The irony was that even though I was making less money than before, I felt more secure. This was a welcome revelation, and came about largely because of the intense Appalachian Trail experience.

Those not in the know might consider long-distance hiking just another form of escapism. But in reality it is just the opposite. Long-distance hikers confront human nature in all its rawness. The immense challenge and deep peace of the wild were irresistible to me.

The Appalachian Trail was far and away the world's best known trail, and had been my one and only goal when I set out to become a hiker in my forties. But while hiking it, I kept hearing experienced hikers marveling about a fantastic jewel of a trail on the West Coast. Given the reverence I held for long journeys on foot, it was probably inevitable that I would turn west for another lifetime adventure.

Chapter 3

The Pacific Crest Trail

It should not be denied that being footloose has always exhilarated us. It is associated in our minds with escape from history and oppression, and with absolute freedom . . . and the road has always led west.

Wallace Stegner
The American West as Living Space

"It's a fabulous trail," everyone told me. "You will love it."

"Unbelievable views," hiker after hiker gushed. In the years leading up to my 2009 attempt to hike the Pacific Crest Trail (PCT), there was unanimity of opinion. It was a great trail.

That begs the obvious question—what makes a "good trail"? The Florida Trail, which runs from Key West to the Florida Panhandle, is not considered by most people to be a very good trail (despite game efforts by committed trail maintainers). It has hundreds of miles of road walking. Besides being boring, the hiker constantly has to resist the temptation to hitchhike. The biggest climb is less than 100 feet.

A good trail, on the other hand, is one with diversity of terrain. By this measure the PCT is not merely a good trail. It is extraordinary. The diversity of its geology is unequaled in any other footpath in the world.

At first glance, the most notable thing about the PCT is its sheer length. It runs from the Mexican to the Canadian border. As the crow flies, that is only a little over 1,000 miles. However, the way the PCT snakes through lake regions and rivers and winds its ways over more than 100 mountain passes, it ultimately measures 2,663.5 miles in length. That makes it *exactly 489 miles longer* than the Appalachian Trail.

The first 703 miles in California are almost entirely *desert*. Even there the hiker is in for a surprise. The trail winds up and down various mountain ranges in the high desert, before dropping steeply down to the desert floor and some of the longest waterless stretches in the United States. This includes the western corner of the famed Mojave Desert.

The Apalachian Trail is primarily a deep-wilderness experience. The signature characteristic of the PCT is broad vistas and wide-open spaces. An aspiring hiker has only one logical choice – do both of them!

The riddle of the PCT, however, comes at mile 703. This is where the trail leaves the desert for good and enters the most renowned part of the PCT—the aptly named *High Sierra*. Here, the trail traverses the crests of the very highest points in the continental United States. For 211 miles the trail doesn't even cross a road, which greatly complicates re-supply.

The upper reaches of the High Sierra are blanketed with snow year round. However, by June 15th, which hikers refer to as *Ray Day*, there has usually been enough snow melt to get through the snowy, icy mountain passes of the High Sierra. Even cutting it this close leaves barely enough time to make it to the Canadian border before the snow starts flying up there in late September or early October.

So it is necessary to thread the needle. A thru-hiker starts in the desert later than is desirable given the scorching heat, and traverses the High Sierra mountain range sooner than is preferable. That challenge—along with the trail's mammoth length—makes it a very difficult trail to thru-hike.

Once through the High Sierra, a thru-hiker has a singular mission—step on it. You consistently have to hike more miles on a daily basis than on the Appalachian Trail. Nonetheless, the trail maintains surprisingly high elevations throughout the rest of California as it passes through, around, or over such delights as Yosemite National Park, Lake Tahoe, and the ski slopes at Squaw Valley.

Finally, the PCT eases up as California's 1,697 miles come to a close. The trail becomes much flatter in Oregon. Unsurprisingly, this is where hikers have traditionally reached deep for their maximum miles. This isn't to say, however, that Oregon is bereft of scenic delights. The trail runs right along the rim of spectacular Crater Lake, and traverses across Mount Hood to Timberline Lodge, all of which help maintain an air of anticipation.

The lowest point on the trail is 140 feet at the Columbia River, which separates Oregon and Washington. Thus, a PCT hiker sees swings in elevation of over 14,000 feet throughout the journey. Once the hiker walks across the Bridge of the Gods into Washington, the trail climbs steadily into the notoriously jagged Cascade Range. The beauty here is rivaled only by the utter desolation the hiker faces.

All PCT veterans agree on one point—be finished before October 1st. The weather in northern Washington is utterly unpredictable thereafter. It was that salient point that would preoccupy me to the point of obsession for the next several months.

***

History is for bitter, old men. Right? Don't worry readers. I don't plan to go through an extensive recitation of the factual history of the PCT. However, a few points are notable.

First, from a preliminary reading of the PCT's history, one is struck by the story's similarity to the conception of the Appalachian Trail. In both cases, there was a Harvard-educated, patrician-like figure who envisioned what many considered a utopian idea. In the case of the Appalachian Trail, it was the ivory-tower personage of Benton MacKaye. Likewise, the PCT was dreamed up by a fellow with an aristocratic-sounding name—Clinton Churchill Clarke.

Both men could be classified as technophobes. "Our youth spend too much time sitting on soft seats in motor cars, too much time sitting on soft seats in movies, and too much time lounging on soft chairs before radios," Clinton Churchill Clarke lamented. "The nation needs a continuous wilderness trail across the United States from Mexico to Canada," Clarke wrote in 1932 to the U.S. Forest Service.

The big difference between the history of the Appalachian Trail and the PCT is very simple. The PCT took a lot longer to complete. The two trails were begun at roughly the same time. Work crews of Boy Scouts played a key early role in carving out PCT sections in the most isolated areas. Nonetheless, while the Appalachian Trail was fully completed by 1937, the much more isolated PCT didn't fully connect all its parts until 1993.

***

The PCT has seen explosive growth over the last decade. The number of Appalachian trail thru-hikers had begun skyrocketing in the late 1990's. Many were finding it practically impossible to adjust back to "the real world", after their journey of a lifetime.

These same people began to hear about the wonders of this new trail in the West.

Specifically, what they heard was how very different it was from the Appalachian Trail. For starters, *there aren't blazes to follow or shelters to sleep in* like the ones that dot the Appalachian Trail. This adds an element of uncertainty to each day. The PCT is considerably more isolated and runs through much wilder terrain. It requires more planning. These hiking pilgrims weren't put off, however. They had gained rock-solid confidence on the Appalachian Trail and lusted after an equivalent or great challenge. Better yet, the PCT is renowned in the tight-knit hiking community for its stunning scenery.

It has now become a virtual rite of passage, once having completed the Appalachian Trail, to immediately begin thinking about attempting the PCT. Some hikers talked about then doing the Continental Divide Trail to achieve the so-called Triple Crown. Others even mentioned getting into mountain climbing. Not me. The PCT was my lone objective. I honestly felt that if I could just thru-hike this trail, then I would have reached my maximum potential as an outdoorsman. I could then rest in peace.

As I was soon to learn, however, success on the Appalachian Trail is by no means a guarantee of success on the Pacific Crest Trail.

BILL WALKER

Chapter 4

The Mexican Border

The only certain freedom is in departure

Robert Frost

"Looks like you're headed the same place as me?" I inquired. Sounds like a pickup line, huh? Well, in a way it was. But what I was looking for was a hiking partner, not a paramour.

It was April 24th, 2009, and I was on a packed bus that was chugging south from San Diego towards the Mexican border. Specifically, I was trying to get to the border town of Campo. But I kept getting conflicting information. Nobody seemed to speak much english. I tried chatting with a couple of these *obreros* (day workers). But none of them had any idea what the Pacific Crest Trail (PCT) was, or exactly where it began.

Fortunately, an Anglican-looking man in his late thirties had come striding to the back of the bus in desert-attire and a new pair of trail running shoes. My mood had lifted, and that's when I had popped the question.

"Yes, mate," he answered pleasantly in a British accent. "There's another fella' up front with a *rucksack* (backpack), as well.

"I'm Skywalker," I said, using my old trail name from the Appalachian Trail.

"St. Rick, here," he offered. As we chatted it became clear that St. Rick was quite a worldly man, having hiked on trails all over the world. He had a polished style, and exuded confidence.

Soon, the other Anglo-American joined us in the back. He was just the opposite from St. Rick—wide-eyed and unsure of himself. He was a marathon runner, but had never hiked. His name was Ralph, and he appeared to be about my age. Before the sun abruptly set on us in the desert that night, it would seem like I knew his entire story.

"My wife just left me for another woman," he lamented. "Nice-looking?" I wondered. Yeah, I know that's not the most helpful thing I could have asked. But whoever said empathy is the strong point of us males?

"You should have heard my father when he found out I was gonna' do this," Ralph recounted incredulously. "The minute my wife picked up the phone, he started screaming, 'What's he doing. We've got to stop him. He's gone crazy.'"

But at the end of the day, Ralph was like any other mortal. Once the idea of hiking the PCT gets lodged in a person's head, sooner or later that person will find himself or herself at the Mexican border.

***

The bus dropped Ralph and me off in the dusty border town of Campo, California. (St. Rick got off early at Lake Morena County State Park to attend the annual PCT *Kickoff Party*). Again, surprisingly few people knew much of anything about the trail.

"What's with this damn place?" I wondered.

"Maybe we're the problem," Ralph offered. "Not them." Once we started hoofing up a large dirt road to the border fence, we learned more about just who we and they are.

Scores of heavily-armored vehicles rushed in and out of a huge border patrol building on our left.

"Man, I'd always thought our border patrol just made a token effort," I said to Ralph. "Kinda' like 'You can't come over, you can't come,' while through winks and nods we were practically waving 'em in."

"Yeah, same here." Over the next few days, as we saw trucks filled with hawkish-looking officials speeding by, and illegals running like their lives depended on it, we'd realize just how mistaken we were.

Finally, at the top of the top of the hill we saw the PCT monument which marks the trail's southern terminus. Just behind it was the double-fenced border.

"About all I can say is let's remember to walk north, not south," I said.

"I'll keep that in mind," Ralph replied dryly.

It was an especially bright day with a dazzling blue sky, as we stood there looking through the fence out into the Mexican desert. It was nothing but barren terrain dotted with tough desert bushes as far as the eye could see. Actually, it didn't look any different than our side of the border. Of course, that shouldn't come as a surprise given that the exact spot we were standing, as well as several hundred miles to our north, were once part of Mexico.

We didn't see any Mexicans, however. That shouldn't have been a surprise, either. Border crashers are like snakes, mountain lions, scorpions, and many other creatures found in the desert—they prefer to travel at night when it's cooler and stealthier. The number of people illegally crossing each year has been estimated at *over a million*. This is despite an immigration quota of seventy-five thousand.

"How far are you looking to go today?" Ralph asked.

"Well, it's over twenty miles to the Kickoff Party," I said. "This late I'll probably just try to get in 12 or 15 miles before dark."

"Yeah, that's kinda' what I was thinking too," he said, which was music to my ears.

"I think the trail goes over that mountain there," I pointed to the left. But ten minutes after starting we found ourselves on a dirt road that didn't appear to lead anywhere except sticky desert bushes.

"Is this right?" I asked.

"Let me go check it out," Ralph said helpfully. He dropped his backpack and started trotting at a brisk jogger's pace through the bushes. A few minutes later he came running back, appearing unwinded.

"Yeah, there's no trail this way," he said.

"Sorry," I offered.

"No worries," he consoled me.

He sure seemed like an agreeable fellow. But we seemed to have two followers and zero leaders in this particular hiking contingent.

***

Hikers may be the nicest folks I ever met. You actually have to look pretty hard to find an asshole. The deep wilderness, as well as the desert, are bound to attract a share of *misanthropes* to be sure. But even these are not usually inflicted with the urge to grate, dominate, condescend, or calculate, which can make humans so unpleasant at times. So I instinctively got a quick lift almost every time I saw other hikers, especially in the back country.

"Oh cool, humanoids," I said to Ralph when we spotted three hikers. Better yet, they had found a rare shaded spot to rest.

"Paul", "Tom", and "Jerry", they introduced themselves.

The first two, Paul and Tom, were flawless physical specimens in their mid-twenties. The third member, Jerry, on the other hand, appeared to have shown up on the PCT gloriously unfit. He was about thirty years old with a baby face, but a matching baby elephant bulging out of his stomach.

"Californians?" I asked.

"No, Detroit," Jerry offered. That was good news. Everybody knows Third World Countries are incubators of nice people. And since Detroit is the closest thing we have in this blessed land to a Third World Country, that was a favorable omen.

"What do ya'll think of the desert so far?" I asked.

"Pretty good," Paul answered.

"You weren't so happy back there when we ran into those two rattlers," Jerry laughed.

"You've already seen two rattlesnakes?" I asked in amazement.

"Yeah," they laughed.

"Today?"

"Yeah, just back there."

"The guidebooks must not have been exaggerating," Ralph said.

***

Ralph's stride was, indeed, that of a marathoner—very little wasted motion. I struggled to keep up. I was maintaining a typical hiker distance of about fifteen feet when he suddenly jumped back towards me. "What's that?"

"Rattler," I said, uncharacteristically knowledgeable.

"Where?" he demanded to know. We began scouring the light brown desert surface. The problem is that rattlers in the desert are predominantly light brown themselves, which probably is no coincidence. Nothing revealed itself—just a steady, but eerie, trilling sound.

"Where is it?" Ralph sounded uncommonly agitated.

"Hell if I know." Finally, after surveying the ground a few minutes, Ralph decided to try to bolt past wherever it was. Just as he started, I saw it.

"There it is," I shouted. "Under the rock."

"Sounds like he's over there," Ralph pointed at a rock.

"Yeah, he's going down a hole," I reported. Ralph started high-stepping to minimize any potential contact.

"I think he's under that rock," Ralph yelled.

"No, no, I'm looking at him," I said excitedly. "Look, look." Soon, the snake had fully slid down the hole.

"I don't hear him anymore," Ralph said confused.

"He went down a hole under a rock," I said relieved.

"Which rock do you think?" he asked.

"No, no, I actually saw him! That rock."

"You saw the rattler?"

"Yeah, definitely a rattler."

"Oh, I didn't know you saw it."

"No worries," I said, in a worried tone.

***

We were seeing everything from blue jeans, to sweaters, to jackets thrown into bushes on the side of the trail.

"Why would somebody get rid of their clothes this early?" I wondered, as we kept seeing garments strewn off to the side of the trail.

"For good reason," Ralph said knowingly.

"Oh, yeah," I caught on. Illegals were stripping them off. This not only helped them cool off, but confuse the border patrol as well.

A person could credibly argue that these people were the best hikers on the trail, given their lack of top notch gear, as well as obstacles faced. But this desperate act of border running shouldn't be glorified one bit. In most cases they risk their lives (approximately 500 illegals per year die in the act of crossing) to get here for one simple reason—economic desperation.

To grow up in Mexico is to have *size envy*. All their lives Mexicans hear tales about the fantastically rich colossus to the north. Specifically, what they hear is about the imperial power stealing one-third of their country in the Mexican-American War (1846-1848). It is historically more complicated than that for the simple reason that Mexico had just obtained these lands itself, upon gaining independence from imperial Spain. They were thinly populated with Mexicans. But Mexican schoolchildren aren't taught that.

There is a common saying in Mexico:

> Poor, poor, Mexico
> So far from God
> So close to the United States.

***

"There is water down at the bottom of this hill," Ralph said.

"Maybe," I cautioned. Here in the desert, it seemed especially important to be conservative.

At the bottom, we found several thirsty hikers, but not even a trickle. The creek bed was dry as a bone.

"Is this the water source?" Ralph asked, incredulously.

"Are you completely out?" asked one hiker.

"No," I responded. "We both have a little."

"Good," he responded with a tone of irony. "We don't need any more drama."

"What happened?" I asked.

"Did you guys see that helicopter come in here earlier?" Ralph and I looked at each other confused.

He then related the tale of two brothers who had gotten here earlier in the day without any water. In fact, they were already badly dehydrated upon arrival. The older brother was apparently in such bad shape that the younger brother (19 years-old) had gone running and calling all over the place trying to find somebody with water. But in the thinly populated desert he couldn't find a soul. So he ran back to his prostrated older brother.

"The older brother hit his SPOT button."

"What's a SPOT button?" I asked.

"You pay about $20 a month for it," he said. "When you hit it, they have your exact location and come get you in a helicopter." The older brother would pick up the trail name, *Chopper* due to this incident, while the younger brother garnered the name, *Savior* for his gallant effort to save his older brother. This was just the beginning. We were to hear much more about their exploits and blunders, all along the way.

"These SPOT buttons sound like James Bond stuff," I laughed. In fact, a few female hikers later told me their parents had made them carry one as a condition of hiking the PCT. But they could be controversial. The previous year a hiker named Lady Bug had come across a rattlesnake in the desert, and leapt onto a boulder for safe haven. There she hit her SPOT button; when the helicopter rescue crew had arrived, they were apoplectic. But then Lady Bug had hit the button again a couple months later, when she broke her leg in northern California.

***

"Whaddya' think?" Ralph asked.

"Do you think there's time to make it to the *Kickoff* tonight?" I asked in a suggestive manner.

"I don't know," he replied, "but if we make it tonight there is bound to be some hot food." That right there should have set off a red flag. How many times had I seen hikers make reckless decisions because they thought it gave them an angle on some hot food?

"We should be able to make it if we go now." We headed off on our first serious climb, as other hikers looked at us curiously from the comfort of their sleeping bags.

Nowhere does the bottom drop out of the temperature like in the desert.

"Hey Ralph," I called ahead as we hurried climbing up the mountain, "I'm stopping to bundle up."

"Me too." A half-hour later, darkness had descended, and we were leaning into a cold, stiff breeze. Worse yet, we were climbing a bare, rocky mountain that offered nowhere feasible to camp.

"My fault," I yelled up to Ralph. "It's unbelievable how quick it got dark."

"No problem," he said, "but I've got to add another jacket." I quickly threw on long-johns and practically everything else. Our breaths were now completely visible. We both put on headlamps and tried to find out where we were on the maps. But it was useless in such a barren area.

"If we keep going we might hear the noise from the *Kickoff*," Ralph suggested.

That became our strategy. But another half-hour later, and we were still climbing, as it got colder and windier. I had hiked 171 days and 0 nights on the Appalachian Trail. Now, here I was my first night on the PCT, hiking practically petrified in the black as pitch night.

"Looks like we're off the trail," Ralph said.

"We could go back down the mountain," I faintly suggested.

But the nighttime adrenaline kept us humping. "Hey," Ralph suddenly said. "Is that a light down there to the left?"

"I see it," I said hopefully. "And that looks like a lake too."

We found ourselves stumbling over rocks and running into various obstacles over the next half-mile. But we finally made it to the Kickoff party. Things were wrapping up for the evening except for some people shivering around a campfire. We had gotten our miles, but not our hot food.

BILL WALKER

Chapter 5

The Kickoff Party

How am I going to get out and take a leak with frozen shoes?

I lay shivering inside my tent, amidst a sea of other tents. As usual, I had awoken in the middle of the night heeding nature's call. The mountain cold settling into this lake valley had plunged the temperature all the way down into the twenties. When I had opened my tent flap and begun clawing around, everything was frozen—the exterior of the tent, the backpack, water bottles, even my shoes. For once, however, I was prepared.

My ever-industrious mother had ordered a light, plastic urine jar from Home Health Care. It's strange how, even in the anonymity of a tent on a freezing cold night, one still can be self-conscious. Nonetheless, this midnight urination came off as planned and saved me an unpleasant midnight rendezvous with the freezing cold. Call it a small confidence-builder, if you will.

Another hiker here in Tent City (we were all later to learn) had awoken with a similar problem. Actually, this woman in her mid-twenties had a bigger dilemma. She needed to have a bowel movement. There was probably a bathroom somewhere in this park, but it was likely a good ways away. And, of course, it was freezing cold. Serendipitously (or so she thought!) though, she had a plastic bag in her tent. I doubt I need to enlighten you as to what brilliant solution she conceived. What the average person may not be aware of, however, is just how difficult such a *crapshoot* can actually be. Here, I must force myself to admit that a month later in a freezing hovel in the Mojave desert, I would consider the exact same course of action as this woman attempted. Quickly, I was to realize the physics of such an act were much more complicated than I had ever fathomed. Plus, I had knowledge of this woman's ill-fated effort at the Kickoff.

Surely, I don't need to tell you the anti-climactic final result of her crapshot. She missed. Needless to say, that led to emergency cleanup action that exposed her to the cold more than if she had just gone outside her tent to begin with.

Missing this once-in-a-lifetime crapshot, however, may not have been her biggest mistake. If you ask me, she made an even bigger blunder the following morning. That's when she told another hiker ("Hey, don't tell anybody, but guess what happened..."). Of course, that hiker did what almost anybody would. She commiserated with the woman before slinking off to tell somebody else. The poor girl who suffered the mishap was soon saddled with the trail name *Shit Bag* for the next 2,600 miles.

***

The Kickoff Party was started in 1999 by a group of ex-hikers to serve as a springboard for the long journey ahead. The weekend is divided between festive eating and drinking, meeting and greeting, and educational seminars on various issues hikers will face along the way. It has been a smashing success.

When I had called to make a reservation a lady had told me, "We hate to turn people back, but we're fully booked."

"Even for thru-hikers?" I asked alarmed. It had seemed like a good place to meet potential hiking partners for the desert. Better yet, it was billed as a butterfly killer.

"Oh no, any thru-hiker can come," she said to my relief. "That's who the party is for."

Even before first light I heard people setting up tables and trays of food in the thirty degree weather. These people were all ex-PCT hikers who probably hadn't been beneficiaries of such *trail magic* during the trail's early years. I had worried that the PCT was just an isolated footpath. To my great delight, though, I was to see countless examples along the way that the PCT is making solid strides at forming its own culture, just like the Appalachian Trail.

***

Hikers just aren't like other people. Any time I'm around lots of long-distance hikers, this truism reveals itself anew. I got to see plenty of them this weekend because the seminars were packed.

At a standing room only seminar on hiker food, a lady with a striking resemblance to the character Major Houlihan on the television show *MASH*, was going on about the importance of continually eating nuts throughout the day.

"Some nuts are better for hikers than other nuts," she emphasized, going into the details of calories, protein intake, etc. She had an innovative teaching style, variously quizzing us on the difficult-to-remember names of various nuts. Finally, she lined up all the nuts together.

"Okay," she barked out. "Which nut works the best for a thru-hiker?"

"The left one," some droll male voice in the back answered without missing a beat. That, of course, brought the house down, including Major Houlihan.

A swaggering fella' of about thirty then took the stage to tell us about hiking in the desert.

"I can't stress enough how important it is to stay hydrated," he kept repeating. "It is much, much easier to stay hydrated than to re-hydrate once you start getting dehydrated." Made sense. The next part, though, stirred up some doubts.

"The best way to do this—trust me on this—is to hike at night." That is the kind of *practical* advice you get from hikers. Incidentally, it was also just the opposite from the counsel you consistently receive from trail guide books, park rangers, and trail bulletin boards. And this guy meant every word of it.

"What about rattlesnakes?" somebody asked. "Aren't they all over the place at night?"

"No doubt about it," he plainly answered. "I can't tell you how many times I've been night-hiking through the desert when I heard that rattling sound and wondered, 'Where is it'? One time a rattler lunged at the girl in front of me. By the way, less than half of rattlesnake bites are deadly."

"Have you ever seen a cougar at night?" I asked him.

"I've heard 'em thrashing around, but never seen one," he answered. "They like to hang out on big rocks and spring out for the clean kill."

"That doesn't scare you?" would have been the logical question. But nobody asked it. It wasn't that type crowd.

Somebody did defensively ask, "What do you recommend doing if you see one?"

"You know in India and countries that have lots of big cat attacks," he answered, "some of the rural people wear hats with bills on both sides because the cats like to attack the back of your neck. If your hat has a bill on both sides, cougars don't know where to attack." That entertaining response brought murmurs of laughter as we all looked at each other in amazement.

"But, honestly," he reasoned when the laughter died down. "Is a cougar really gonna' look at something moving six-feet of the ground with a light shining off the top of its head and think, 'There goes my next meal'?"

"I don't think so," he added in a reassuring tone. I'll have to hand it to him. The reason we were all at the Kickoff was to hear what it's really like out there, not some hedged remarks in cover-your-ass language.

The seminar ended when a man who looked to be pushing seventy sincerely asked, "I've never tried a thru-hike. How do you get your trail name?"

"What's your real name?"

"Bob Atkinson," the man responded.

"Well, Blow-Job Bob hasn't been taken yet," he replied logically. The seminar broke up in stitches, and we all filed out.

***

A well-known trail angel named Meadow Mary (married to the even better-known hiker, Billy Goat) had a booth set up to give massages to hikers hoping to iron out any kinks before heading off into the desert. All the predictably idiotic jokes aside, the massages were anything but kinky. Rather, hikers kept emerging from there looking like they had gone fifteen rounds with Mike Tyson.

The next morning the former hikers served us yet another fabulous breakfast, while a volunteer went around passing out a very critical piece of paper to each hiker. It containined the most up-to-date information available about the water sources in the desert. Then, I joined the northward-bound masses fanning out into the desert.

Chapter 6

The Desert

The desert is atonal, cruel, clear, neither romantic nor classical.
Like death? Perhaps. And that is why life nowhere appears so
brave, so bright, so full of miracle as in the desert.

Edward Abbey, *Desert Solitaire*

The summer of 1942 was the very darkest hour of the Second World War. The British, despite their vast experience in desert warfare, had been shocked when the Germans sacked their fortress at Tobruk in the Sahara Desert. Suddenly, the United States had been thrust into desert warfare against the *Desert Fox* himself, Erwin Rommel. Despite the vast desert regions in our own homeland, the United States was utterly lacking in desert warfare experience.

One of the first things the U.S. military did was hire Edward Adolph, a professor at the University of Rochester, to commission a study on how much water soldiers required in desert warfare. Adolph commenced a series of studies on water deprivation in which he variously locked people in jeeps all day in the glaring sun, marched them in the day, at night, etc. The results were not encouraging.

"We find that a man who stops drinking water sweats about as fast as one who continues to drink," Adolph found. Since the human brain is about 75% water, we can keep on sweating without drinking water. However, after a few hours a person begins to lose his or her mental faculties.

"All the evidence known at present shows that a man cannot do without water, nor be trained to do with less water."

Adolph's research was groundbreaking at the time of World War II, and to this day remains the gold standard on human water requirements.

***

Every year about two hundred people die in our national parks. They drown, they fall, have heart attacks, drive off cliffs, you name it. But few ever die as strangely as 26 year-old David Coughlin.

In the summer of 1999, David and his friend, Raffi Kodikian headed out on that great American rite of passage—the cross-country road trip. They left from Boston and on day six arrived at Carlsbad Caverns National Park in the Chihuahuan desert in southern New Mexico. First, they went to the ranger station to inquire as to the cheapest place they could camp. The ranger recommended a campsite in an area called *Rattlesnake Canyon*. Specifically, they were to drive down a dirt road, park their car, and walk a mile down to the campsite on the desert floor. Raffi filled out their campsite permit for a stay of *one day*.

The ranger also advised them to carry at least one gallon of water for each day they planned to be out there. David and Raffi were on tight budgets, however, and chose to purchase just three pint bottles for the two of them. They hurried out to make it to the campsite before dark.

They easily found the parking lot for Rattlesnake Canyon, strapped on their backpacks, and soon reached the bottom of the canyon floor. They had planned to camp right there, but were in an adventuresome mood. So David and Raffi took a turn onto a lightly traveled trail which they followed for about a mile. Here they set up camp

All was well.

***

David and Raffi broke camp early the next morning to avoid getting caught in the broiling sun. Quickly they realized they were lost.

Because of its shear vastness, hiking in the desert can be tricky. David and Rafffi spent the afternoon wandering thirstily in various directions hoping vainly to come across water somewhere. But wisely they elected to not wander too far afield. They reasoned that since they had filled out the camping permit for only one day, somebody would soon come looking for them.

That night around midnight their hopes were suddenly lifted when both spotted a light on the far canyon wall. *There must be a road over there*, they reasoned. The following morning they began scaling a steep incline to try to find the road. Altogether, it took three hours in the blazing heat to arrive at the top. Once at the top, it became immediately clear there was no road anywhere around. But that wasn't the worst part.

The previous day, David Coughlin and Raffi Kodikian had actually played it pretty smart by seeking shade and not using up too much bodily water. But the trek they had just made to the top of the shelf probably used up as much as eight times the bodily water than if they had laid low. And it left them on barren heights completely exposed. This is when things began to get ugly.

***

Vultures started circling over David and Raffii. Like almost everyone else, they had seen old westerns in which vultures wait until their prey is too weak to resist. At that point, the vultures strike.

"They were probably about thirty feet above us," Raffi later testified. "It would start with just one circling and then another one would come and then another one. They would just stick around and watch us. We would wave our arms to let them know that we were still alive. My understanding of buzzards at the time was that *they start* before you're done—as soon as you're too tired to fight them." David and Raffi happened to be disastrously wrong on this point. Vultures are actually highly social creatures that like to hang out around outdoors people, as well as other vultures.

They decided to head back into the canyon they had used up so much effort climbing out of earlier in the morning. First, though they found some pieces of cactus bush and began trying to suck water out of it. Since cacti absorb water, this theoretically could have helped. But they remained desperately thirsty. Now it was time to try the oldest trick in the book.

They would each drink their own urine. Had they known better, however, they would never have tried it. A person's body actually uses up more water processing the urine's waste than it gains from the liquid. Nonetheless, they filled up their pint bottles with urine which was a dark gold color, sampled it, and immediately gagged. David now began to stagger and it was all they could do to get back to their tents.

"We will not let the buzzards get us alive," Raffi wrote in their journal on August 7th, the hottest day yet. "God forgive us." Then they decided on a ghastly course of action. They would each slit the other's wrist. They pulled out their one knife and each took a turn at carving the other's blood vessels. But, for whatever reason—fear, weakness, whatever—neither was able to do more than mark up the other person's wrists. Now they were faced with having to take everything the desert could throw at them in a slow, agonizing final act.

David began vomiting uncontrollably. Soon he was begging Raffi to kill him. Assuming they were both going to die, Raffi decided to oblige his friend. He took the knife out and tried to stab David in the chest. The first attempt was only partly successful. But on the second stab he achieved deep penetration into David's heart, who started bleeding profusely.

"Pull it out," David then said.

"I asked him if he was in pain," Raffi later testified. "He said he felt better and smiled." Raffi held David's hand and put a tee-shirt over his head as David died. He then went back into his tent to await his own fate.

Several hours later he heard footsteps. Ranger Lance Mattson approached the remnants of Raffi's tent and was shocked to see someone in there.

"Please tell me you have water," Raffi rasped.

"Yes, I do," replied the ranger. "Is everything okay?"

"Why weren't you here earlier?" was Raffi's croaking reply. The ranger handed Raffi a bottle of water, which he began, at turns, inhaling and vomiting.

"Where's your buddy?" the ranger asked.

"Over there," Raffi said, gesturing to a makeshift stone grave he had constructed. Matson saw nothing as he wandered around.

"Where?" he asked again.

"Right here," Raffi pointed out. "I killed him," he said calmly.

***

The facts above come from the sometimes rambling journal they kept, as well as the testimony Raffi delivered under oath. The police, however, flat out didn't buy it.

"I don't care what anyone says," the county sheriff said. "You just don't do that to your best friend."

An equally skeptical county prosecutor stated, "You don't get to kill someone in the state of New Mexico just because they ask you to." One story that gained currency was that David Coughlin had trysted with Raffi's ex-girlfriend, Kirsten Swan. The theory was that at some point in their traumatic journey David had confessed to Raffi, at which point Raffi became enraged.

Raffi Kodikian pleaded guilty to second-degree murder and put his fate in the hands of the court.

"It was mercy, not mental illness, that made you kill him?" the judge asked.

"What I thought I was doing," Raffi replied, "was keeping my friend from going through 12 to 24 hours of hell before he died." David's parents believed Raffi, and publicly supported him, while Raffi's parents sat there weeping. Raffi listened intently. The judge sentenced Raffi to a lighter than expected 24 months, of which he served 16 months before being released for good behavior.

This whole tale, which reads like a Greek tragedy, is brilliantly recounted in Jason Kersten's book, *Journal of the Dead—A Story of Friendship and Murder in the Desert.* Kersten actually tells the story in a way that lends a kind of poignant dignity to the whole drama.

The dread that so many people feel in the desert is not usually through imminent danger. Rather, it is something far worse—the desert's implacable indifference. We are humans and our bodies are full of water. The desert will efficiently and inexorably suck it out of us. In the process, we become deranged.

The message for the desert hiker is loud and clear—*caveat emptor.*

Chapter 7

And They're Off

Bliss was in that dawn to be alive.

William Wordsworth

It was a brilliant pageantry of spirited, clean, well-fed, well-hydrated hikers in their desert best that bounded out of Lake Morena County State Park in southern California with such high hopes. The PCT had issued a record number of hiking permits (over 500) to thru-hiking hopefuls this year. And, of course, many had already picked up colorful trail names ranging from Heartless Bastard, to Helen of Troy (well, nice try anyway), to Serial Killer.

To describe us as heavily laden would be an understatement. I was carrying about 42 pounds which was a dozen more than I had begun with on the Appalachian Trail. Specifically, we had been advised to carry winter clothes all the way through the desert, which had our backpacks bulging. Attached or stashed in each backpack was a minimum of four liters of water.

I had always wondered why Arabs in the Middle East wear such long robes. *Wouldn't that Saudi royal family be more comfortable in Izod golf shirts?* But once in the desert, I quickly began to understand. Those robes are light and loose, and provide maximum protection from the sun. Most hikers, male and female, were wearing long-sleeved, beige Sahara desert shirts. *Yogi*, whose PCT Handbook is the one indispensable guide to hiking the PCT, had strongly advised, "Get yourself the widest, dorkiest hat you can find." Everybody seemed to have taken that advice to heart. On our heads were widebrimmed white fedoras with chin straps to cover our faces and nose.

When we passed through the Boulder Oaks Campground at mile six, a crowd was gathered around the faucet, drinking like camels.

"Let me have some," a healthy-looking, squarely-built girl in her mid-twenties immediately exclaimed upon seeing me. She wasn't talking about my water, though, but my height.

"Just take steps like this," I stretched out as far as I could. "You'll be in Canada before you know it." This generated the intended laughter, to be sure. All weekend at the Kickoff, I had been hearing, "God I wish I had your height." But I was uncomfortable with the high expectations it created.

"I'm Galit," this girl introduced herself.

"Where are you from?" I asked, noticing a foreign accent.

"Israel." Those Israelis sure didn't win all those wars by being shrinking violets.

I lay down in the shade next to some other guy with our backpacks as headrests.

"Hey guys, watch out for those bees," Galit said. I jumped up, suddenly alarmed at the swarm of bees all over my back. Galit immediately jumped in and started fanning wildly at the bees to get them off our backs.

This girl reminded me a little of myself. She was probably a bit insecure about what lay ahead and was looking for hiking partners. Something told me she would find them. Indeed, she soon had herself embedded with a big group that got dubbed the *International Brigade*.

***

Perhaps my hiking contingent should have been called *the Sausage Brigade*. There were four males, aged 39, 48, 48, and 66. The latter, Dave—to my surprise—had called my name out at the

Kickoff.

"I bought your book at the book signing at Borders in Sarasota," he had said.

"Oh yeah," I remembered.

"It was my inspiration to come out here and give it a whirl," he then claimed. *That* was surely an exaggeration. But it did make me feel obligated to hang together with him, for at least awhile. His heart and soul were in this hike, and he had obviously trained meticulously.

Dave had been ripping to go that morning. As the rest of us scurried around to get packed up, he toodled around with his backpack firmly strapped on. That was a no-no. It expends unnecessary energy. His biggest mistake, though, was the classic rookie error. His backpack looked like he had stuffed the kitchen sink in there somewhere. It weighed about 50 pounds, and quickly earned him the trail name, '*Lighten Up*'.

A pattern soon developed. Ralph, St. Rick, and I would hike a couple miles, notice Dave wasn't back there, and stop for a rest. When Dave would arrive huffing and puffing fifteen minutes later, the four of us would head on. But only three of us would be rested.

These breaks did afford us a chance to view a few of our new colleagues. An athletic-looking redheaded girl in her thirties that I had seen at the Kickoff came by.

"Excuse me," I playfully said, "but the three of us are all out of water. Could we borrow some of yours?"

"No," she immediately barked out and quickly jumped into a fighting crouch. "Me do kung-fu." The short, squatty guy trailing behind her must have appreciated it because he broke into a delirious laugh. He named her *Kung-Fu*, and she dubbed him *Giggles*. Both names stuck all the way.

We soon passed Kung-Fu alone on the side of the trail.

"How about coming along to help us not get lost," I suggested.

"Well, I'll hike with you for awhile," she said grudgingly. These women out here sure were a different breed from what I had grown up with in the Deep South. In place of charm and subtle calculation, you often got bluntness and fierce independence.

Perhaps trying to assert my own self, I bolted ahead of the group down a long, sandy straightaway.

"Skywalker, Skywalker," they all suddenly were shouting. *Oh God, snake!* I started frantically high-stepping as fast as I could for about twenty yards. But they all kept screaming my name. I turned around and looked at the ground, but saw nothing. Instead, all my amused comrades were pointing to the fork in the trail I had just missed. *Be careful.* Rattlesnakes were bound to give anybody this side of Huck Finn the creeps. But the lack of landmarks in the desert probably makes getting lost the greater threat. Every year there are hikers that pick up the trail names Wrongway or Backtrack.

The trail angels and hiking community, having spoiled us at the Kickoff, apparently decided to slowly wean us. When we got to Kitchen Creek Road at mile ten, a couple of trail angels from the Kickoff had pulled up in vans. Coolers full of ice-cold drinks and snacks were laid out for us.

The best part, though, came when a guy named Hector interrupted my reclining reverie. "You're next, Skywalker." Hector was famous in PCT circles as *The Foot Doctor*. He had me soak them in some concoction for a few minutes and then propped them up in his lap to examine them.

"Wonderful calluses," he said approvingly. "These things can take some punishment." Talk about an ego boost. Heck, telling a hiker he has great foot calluses at the beginning of a twenty-six hundred mile hike, is the greatest possible benediction.

***

The vague, Hollywood-inspired image many of us had of the desert was of a hot, flat cakewalk. However, immediately we received a jolt. The trail wound its way almost three thousand feet up a mountain. The sun was dipping below the horizon when we got near the top.

"I believe everybody is headed to *Cibbet Flats*," St. Rick said. That sounded pretty good—lots of people. Dave should be able to make it there. And Cibbet Flats should be flat. Right? Not even close. When we turned the corner, there was a hiker's version of a mob scene. Worse yet, Cibbet Flats was a ravine, with a filthy-looking stream bisecting its banks. Nonetheless, people were planning to stay here, and the least angular spots were already dotted with pitched tents and sleeping bags.

"I'm gonna' give this a miss," St. Rick said in British parlance.

"Oh wow," I moaned. "This is Dave's first time ever camping, and we're already leaving him behind."

"Yeah, I feel bad, too," agreed Ralph.

"First night out here—you two guys abandon him and he gets eaten by a cougar," St. Rick piped in with his very correct English accent. But as I had long known, long-distance hikers do habitually leave each other behind. I was no different. We had a long journey ahead.

It was getting cold and windy and we were faced with an exposed climb to try to get to Burnt Rancheria Campground. I left word with a couple hikers to tell Dave that we were moving on. Dave ended up hiking until dark and made it to this last ravine. He had then attempted to set up camp on this incline for the first time in his 66 years. In the middle of the night his tent blew down and he spent the rest of the night keeping it erected. His troubles were just beginning.

Ralph, St. Rick, and I headed up the mountain, trying to beat dark. Unlike a couple nights before, we made it to the campground just before dark. However, the wind dominated the landscape, and the three of us ended up pitching our tents hundreds of yards apart in the most bizarre places. Oh, how I missed the shelters of the AT.

After 22 miles I reasoned I deserved a hot meal. I pulled out my old alcohol stove and tried to generate a flame. But one time after another, the cold wind harassed the modest flame my stove could generate. *Hmm. So this is how all these forest fires get started out here?* I finally gave up and ate cold food.

This trail is going to take some getting used to.

Chapter 8

Trout Lily

"Man, you should have seen this Mexican dude," she exclaimed. "He just came out of nowhere and started begging me for water."

"In Spanish?" I asked.

"No, perfect English," she said in wonderment.

"You should have asked him to hike with you," I suggested.

"I thought about it. I swear I did. But I don't want to get in any shit with these border officials."

Some people just have star quality, pure and simple. This girl had it from the get-go. I say girl. She was 29, but probably got carded every time she ordered a beer due to her youthful bounciness.

She was hot. Okay, everybody's hot in the desert, right? No, she was the real deal. Great figure, a million dollar smile, a southern accent to make you swallow your heart, and—it also seemed like— cool as hell. I had seen her razzing around at the Kickoff (who hadn't!) and wondered if she was a hiker or a partier. She was both.

"I'm Trout Lily," she introduced herself to her mostly male audience.

"Where are you from?" I asked, resume talk being the domain of the lame and unimaginative.

"Memphis, but I live in Hood River, Oregon."

"Wow, everybody I'm meeting is from Oregon."

"Yeah," she laughed. "we're all escapists." Good line, even if it is true.

"My parents were totally pissed when I told them about this," she confided to this crowd of theretofore strangers. That quality of openness would serve her in good stead in the reigning trail culture.

"I move back home to Memphis every few years, decide I can't live there anymore, and then head off with my dog in my pickup truck to places like Asheville, Hood River, or *Antarctica.*"

"Antarctica?" I exclaimed. "What the hell did you do there?"

"Worked in the kitchen?"

"Did you like it?"

"It got boring," she said. "All people did was drink and have sex."

"What's so boring about that?"

"I mean," she laughed, "you just had to see it. They filled the jars in the men's *and* women's bathroom with condoms. The janitor told me she had to refill 'em every morning." So far, Trout Lilly was checking all the boxes of the perfect trail iconoclast.

"Have you ever hiked before?" I asked.

"Yeah, I did the AT a few years before." That figured. I'd already spotted her on the trail a few times and wondered what she was up to. One place you'd see her jiving with people; the next time she'd be galloping along.

"I've only done three miles today," she said. "I've gotta' get goin'." That was her style—entertain a little while and then get on with it. She was bound to be a formidable presence.

Everybody took a side trail at mile 44 to get to the Mount Laguna Post Office. By the time I got there it looked like hikers had formed a sit-in inside the post office. Stove, clothes, cameras, food, shoes, tents—you name it, people were sending it either to a post office further up the trail or all the way home. In some cases people had bought the wrong thing. Others were shedding weight as fast as they could. Worried about setting the desert on fire, I bounced my stove 660 miles forward to Kennedy Meadows.

Unfortunately, one of the hikers tooling around the post office had a different mission. Just Jack was 68 years old, and coming off a gutsy southbound thru-hike of the AT the previous year, that had taken him eight months. This year he had shown up at the Kickoff looking to pull another rabbit out of the hat. Unfortunately, an asthma condition was driving him nuts in the desert.

"The desert's not for me," he simply said.

"Hate to see you go," everybody sincerely told him. He had already distinguished himself with his delightful cracker barrel sense of humor.

"I'm not going anywhere," he said. He bought a car and started following the bubble of hikers to the various trail towns, and soon was the most popular person on the trail.

***

The PCT considers shelters a sissy, East-Coast thing; the trail figureheads take great pride in their bootstrap philosophy. But if there is one single place on the entire trail they ought to build a shelter, it's at the Pioneer Mail Campsite. It is dominated by gunshot winds that come barreling over the horizon.

There was absolutely nowhere else to camp here that remotely offered any protection from the wind. Trout Lily and another girl sought cover in a ditch down the hill, even though they were unable to set up their tents down there. Thereafter, anytime she was in a bad mood, we accused her of being *ditchy*.

I tried pitching my tent in a different ditch from the one where Trout Lily was hiding. But it wasn't even remotely level, and I finally decided to erect it right next to St. Rick's tent, hoping his would create a windshield. However, it was impossible to set up alone, as the wind bullied the various parts of the tent all over the place.

"Hey Rick," I called into his tent. "Could you just help hold this thing in place for a second." It was embarrassing to ask for help. But I was a realist. St. Rick jumped out of his tent, hammered away at some stakes, and was back in his tent within a minute. He always played it smart.

All I could do now was jump in my tent, put on my maximum of seven layers, and hunker down for a sleepless night. The dominant melody of the evening was these gunshot winds moaning a dreary tune.

***

Was the desert ugly or beautiful? That quickly became a matter of heated debate.

I got my first taste of truly *high desert* the next morning, and it rocked me big-time. The minute I cleared the ridge from the campsite, I was confronted with a breathtaking landscape. A cold wind clobbered me for miles while walking on an exposed ridge. Nonetheless, after hating the desert all frigid night long, I was suddenly enraptured. Mesas, canyons, red cliffs, and arid tablelands extending out into the distance stood out in high relief. To me, it is these vast open spaces that give the American West the overwhelming feeling of unbounded freedom.

*The high desert proved very different from my
pre-conceived image of the desert.*

After several miles I descended again to the more familiar low desert. About the only thing they had in common, as far as I could tell, was their overwhelming aridity. Fortunately, there was a well. But the water looked grotesque.

"What the hell," I said peering down into it.

Big John came over and examined it. "Yeah, all the muck has risen to the top."

"But look at the bottom," I said. "There's crap everywhere down there too."

"I guess you just have to get it out of the middle," he said good-naturedly. I pulled out my filter, carefully placing the tip of the funnel right in the middle, and started pumping.

Despite its relative simplicity, the low desert wears its own veil of mystery.

"Life is not crowded upon life as in other places," wrote Edward Abbey, in his classic tome, *Desert Solitaire*, "but scattered abroad in spareness and simplicity, with a generous gift of space for each herb and bush and tree. Abbey staunchly maintained that, in fact, there is no shortage of water in the desert. There was just the right amount of water to insure open, generous spacing between plants and animals, and even homes, towns, and cities. The problem came, according to Abbey, when you built giant cities where they shouldn't be (sorry Las Vegas and Phoenix!). This growth for the sake of growth was a cancerous, obsessive, madness.

Abbey, himself, had been a park ranger and probably knew of water sources in the desert that no other human did. But he also said that there were magical springs that only animals knew. At night the mammals came—first deer, next bobcats, followed by cougars, and finally coyotes—to drink, not to kill.

Later in the day, I dropped to the *desert floor* for the first time. There stood the most well-known symbol of the desert— the cactus bush. It's the toughest, most well-fortified plant imaginable, and I could only guess how long each one has been standing. Perhaps centuries; perhaps millennia.

I had been alone the last few hours, but as the sun fell I ran into an attractive Canadian girl setting up her tent just off the trail. *What is it about these trails that all the girls are so attractive?* Maybe it was because the PCT had only one girl for every four guys (The AT was probably 2.5 to 1). I honestly don't know. In any event, this was the same girl whose tent I had accidentally poked my head into last night at the Pioneer Mail Trailhead, thinking it was St. Rick's tent. So she must have been wondering just who the hell this 'peeping hiker' was who always turned up, wherever she happened to be, at bedtime.

"Kinda' cool the way you can just pull off to the side of the trail here in the desert and set up camp," I said.

"Yeah well, I seem to remember some ridges," she laughed. There was a spot right next to hers to set up my tent. Having already hiked twenty miles, I thought about it. But I decided otherwise. *Hike your own hike* was the fundamental paradigm amongst hikers. So I headed on.

The most pleasant hour in the desert is at sundown, after the awful heat of the afternoon. The sinking desert sun resembles a flaming globe and leaves behind fanciful lipstick sunsets. It was very pleasant following the trail as it serpentined through countless cactus bushes. A few minutes before dark, I simply pulled five yards off the trail to set up camp. I did have one concern, however.

There were holes everywhere. *Rattlesnakes.* So I wandered around grabbing big rocks to put over all the nearby holes, marveling at my improvisation. However, somebody later told me this wouldn't thwart a determined snake from surfacing.

"How do rattlers get water in the desert?" I had asked.

"They burrow down in the holes and drink the blood of the rodents they find down there." This was the time of day they liked to emerge.

Sleeping near snake holes is simply a fact of life in the low desert though, and I occupied myself in my tent pulling scores of burrs out of my socks.

Chapter 9

Caches, Ledges, and Trail Repartee

Ten by ten was the thru-hiker's motto in the desert. The idea was to try to hike ten miles by ten o' clock in the morning, then maybe eke out a few more miles before noon. At that point a hiker should spend several hours under any possible shade he or she can find. The reasoning was that you used up so much water during the middle of the day, that the miles you gained from it aren't worth it. Then, at 4:00 or so, you should resurrect yourself and hike until dark. It made sense. But would I really want to just lie under some bush for several hours in the middle of the day?

World's most important resource. The average hiker like myself might not even attempt the PCT without dedicated trail angels stashing water caches.

I was in the middle of a 24 mile waterless stretch, followed by another 25 mile waterless run. The only water re-supply in that 49 miles was at Scissor Crossing. And it was not a natural water source. Rather, it was a *cache*. At the Kickoff, the speakers had repeatedly reinforced the point that we should carry enough water to get by in case the cache is not stocked.

Nonetheless, like most hikers I arrived at Scissor's Crossing low on water, and high on expectations. Some trail angel, or maybe an entire trail club, had built a sturdy construction of wooden cabinets. Inside, were scores of gallon containers of water. The rule of thumb is to take only what you need. But there was so much water here, I was able to chug all I wanted and lug several liters with me into the rugged San Felipe Hills. Being so well hydrated, I decided to go ahead and tackle the mid-day desert sun.

Here, the trail took on a different character as it inexorably wound its way up a barren mountain. Soon, I found myself out on a narrow ledge along a steep canyon. Ledge walking takes some getting used to; it was easy to become anxious and hurry. But patience was the real virtue because these ledges often went on for miles. Finally, the trail did a sharp u-turn and next thing I knew I was out on another ledge walking in the opposite direction, not that far from the ledge I had just been on.

A break would have been nice, but there was absolutely no shade at all in the middle of the day. So I just kept hiking nakedly exposed to the full wrath of the sun. The only thing I could do now was continually drink a lot of water, hoping to ward off that silent visitor—dehydration. My goal was to make it to another water cache by this evening.

Finally, I saw the lonely figure of Jerry, a member of the threesome from Detroit. To the naked eye, it was apparent his bulging gut had already deflated, due to monsoon-like perspiration. He was once again digging deep to try to keep up with his two friends.

"Man, I *really* don't like this," he said in as friendly of a way that a complaint can be registered.

All I could offer was a dry-throated cliché: "Hang in there."

A mile further up I came upon his two partners, Tom and Paul, sitting in a crouch on the ledge. I immediately dropped to as supine of a position as my almost 7 feet could manage on the narrow ledge —head up against granite backstop, butt on the hot trail surface, and feet dangling off the cliff.

"How long have ya'll been waiting?" I asked.

"About a half-hour," Tom said. I was impressed while chatting with them that they didn't use the occasion to gripe at Jerry for his tardiness.

"You know, these things usually work themselves out," I said, broaching the subject that was surely on their minds. "The *trail* actually decides who you eventually end up hiking with."

"Well, there is another issue involved," Tom said diplomatically. "Jerry is a manager at the outfitter where we all work in Detroit. He decides if we get hired back."

They stayed together.

***

Some hikers swear that their fellow hikers get to know more about them than their boyfriends and girlfriends. Whether or not that is an exaggeration, one thing is undeniable. You bond deeply, and often instantaneously, out there.

I finally got to the campsite I had hoped for and my mood immediately lifted. Another trail angel had driven dozens more gallons of water up a jeep road. The person had tied a thin rope through each jug and around a tree to keep it all tidy.

Better yet, Trout Lily was one of those on hand. The topics of shoe brands, backpack weight, food, water, snow levels, blisters, etc. get saturated during the daytime hours. As has been known to happen at campsites, the conversation turned to the opposite sex. I had been living in Florida for two years before coming out for the PCT, and treated them to some fare of Florida-style dating.

"I was dating a woman almost twenty years older than me down there," I said.

"Nuh, uh," Trout Lily said in disbelief.

"What else are you gonna' get in South Florida," I said. "At least she didn't live in a damn nursing home."

"But then one day I'm strolling along the beach and run into this girl (Liz) half my age—24 years old to be exact. She had trained all her life to make the Olympic swimming team, but missed it. That was it. Next thing you know she's gone from an ascetic lifestyle to drinking and dating older men. She really didn't know how to handle either.

"After several months of going out with Liz, I'm walking on the beach with the older lady who had morphed into my friend. All of a sudden, this older guy walks up with an alarmed look on his face, and says, 'Bill Walker?'. 'Yeah', I answered. He grabbed me by my elbows and says, 'come with me'. 'Can I bring this lady with me?' I asked. 'No', he said. 'I want to talk with you'. I'm thinking, *what the hell is happening here.*

"'I'm Liz's father', he proceeds to tell me. 'She died in her sleep last night with her ex-boyfriend'. Liz had just told me the week before that this same ex-boyfriend—who was 62 years old—had stalking tendencies. So that's Florida-style dating for you."

"Sounds like swapping out Florida for the PCT was a good trade," Too Obtuse incisively observed.

Trout Lily didn't blanch one bit.

"I date this big, old surfer. I swear he's got the most unbelievable body. I can't quit thinking about it."

After listening to her rhapsodically describing his many bona-fides as a modern-day Romeo, she said, "But he keeps having sex with his ex-girlfriend."

Nobody said anything, so she added, "I don't care, though. I just wish I didn't have to pay his rent."

Poor fella'. Life sure is a bitch. Unfortunately, however, this same guy was to play a seminal role in derailing Trout Lily from the PCT.

Chapter 10

Seeds of Disaster

There are three things in life you don't want to do:

1. Play poker with somebody named 'Slim'.
2. Buy a Rolex from somebody who is out of breath.
3. Go hiking in the desert with a pair of shoes that are too small.

A PCT hiker, who wasn't even a nerd, could write an entire book on shoes. The treadway is very different from the Appalachian Trail, especially in the desert. For that reason, most people wear trail running shoes. They were breathable for starters (if you have the right damn size!). And they were lighter, so you could go further. But Yogi and others repeatedly stressed that your shoes had to be at least one size bigger than you normally wear.

It's the one decision you have to get right from the beginning, and I had gotten utterly neurotic beforehand about it. Yet, I still ended up screwing it up. I'm normally a 13 ½ so I had ordered Vasque Size 14 low cuts. But the minute I tried them on, they had felt snug. I checked the REI website, but 14 was the largest size they offered for Vasque shoes. Like many hikers, I thought REI was the center of the hiking universe. If they didn't have size 15, then I assumed Vasque didn't make Size 15 shoes. This would prove to be a grievous blunder.

I had wandered with my backpack all over the beach in Florida in that pair of size 14 shoes. One day I'd think they were big enough; the next day I'd change my mind. Not until the day before I left did I make a final decision to wear the Vasque Size 14's. *Maybe they'll stretch* had been the final tiebreaker.

Now here I was in the worst of the desert heat. The temperature in the sun was well over 100 degrees. But the ground surface temperature was probably in the neighborhood of 140 degrees. It was like a modified version of walking on coals, and turned hikers into kangaroos. But instead of my shoes stretching as I had hoped, it was my *feet*.

It was becoming more and more clear that I had a serious problem. I was alternating between one and two pairs of socks, trying band-aids, mole skin, duct tape, elevating them on breaks, you name it. For good or for bad, I was even trying different ways of taking steps. But my feet honestly felt like a furnace. This was alarming. Hot and moist are the perfect breeding conditions for blisters.

Actually, all kinds of people were having foot problems. One girl picked up the name *Blister Sister*, and another guy was called *Dead Man Walking* due to the blisters ringing his feet.

"It's knees that knock people off the AT," hiking veteran Too Obtuse said. "But feet are what knock people off the PCT." However, it wasn't my feet that were the problem. They had held up fabulously on the AT. It had to be the shoes. And I sure as heck wasn't going to find any size 15 trail shoes in any of these backwater trail towns.

I took a side trail to the tiny resort of Warner Springs, hoping for a miracle. I ran into several hikers, in an air-conditioned restaurant there. Afterwards, as several of us were limping through a parking lot, St. Rick noted, "Gosh, mates. We're supposed to be walking to Canada, but people can barely make it through the bloody parking lot."

***

Trout Lily and I headed out of Warner Springs in the late afternoon, hoping to make several miles before dark. After several miles, we came to the banks of Agua Caliente Creek.

"Looks like a perfect place to camp," I said.

But Trout Lily was dubious. "I don't know if I should keep goin' or stay here," she said.

"There's a climb out of here," I said. "You might get stuck on a ridge."

"I haven't done enough miles," she muttered. For all her scintillating qualities, she seemed to be genuinely insecure. I left her alone and intentionally set up my tent well apart from hers.

By the Book showed up at dark. As his trail name might suggest, he was one of these people who had delved into every imaginable minutiae of equipment and trail planning. One nice thing about having Trout Lily around was I knew he'd train his total attention on her, and I'd be spared a seminar on all these mind-numbing topics.

This was a phenomenon I'd see over and over along the trails. By the Book was a pudgy, non-descript, middle-aged man with ruddy cheeks and the least likely possible suitor (with the possible exception of me!) of Trout Lily. Yet he was on her like a metal to a magnet for the rest of the night until she finally pleaded fatigue and went to sleep. There's something about the trail that demands the release of infatuation with members of the opposite sex, even when lust is out of the question. It was up to the precious few women out here to put up with it. Many, of course, played it to their advantage, and Trout Lily could do that with the best of 'em. But sometimes it apparently just became too much for them.

The very next night, after a big group of males plus Trout Lily had hiked twenty miles and finally gotten to our intended campsite, Trout Lily simply announced, "I'm going on." Everybody seemed to get the message, because nobody offered to join her. There wasn't much of anywhere for her to camp, according to the map. Indeed, when she did finally camp her tent blew down several times during what turned out to be a miserable evening. But at least it got her the hell away from us!

***

The British have a core contradiction in their character. As an island nation they can be annoyingly insular. Yet that same island nation had once ruled over the greatest empire the world has ever seen. Centuries of this have made the British both competent in foreign affairs, as well as arrogant. They really do understand foreign cultures better than most Americans do. And it drives them crazy to have to perennially play second fiddle to us daft Yanks.

St. Rick was a classic Englishman in so many ways. As we walked along this Saturday afternoon, it seemed like he had hiked all over the globe. Because of his rock-solid confidence, he never hurried things. I stayed right on his heels listening to his colorful descriptions of his journeys.

"Why are you doing that?" Americans often ask, about a long hike I'm planning. That is not a question that a Brit, or a European for that matter, is likely to hear. Outdoor vacations are a much more integral and valued part of their life.

"It is a source of embarrassment to me," St. Rick confided, "that as well as I've always been treated over here, the way my countrymen take so long to warm up toward Americans."

"The core of the problem," a British guy once confided in me, "is that we just can't quite get over the idea that we're smarter than you are." I told St. Rick that story.

"We have stupid people too," he said. "We just don't put 'em all over television talk shows and everywhere like you do here."

Our discussion was now becoming too abstract. But I will stick with the thesis that if outdoor vacations (they can be quite economical— Rick was a social worker in London. On the Appalachian Trail I hiked extensively with a janitor from London named English Bob) became a greater part of American culture, we would begin to understand the world better. Better yet, the world could actually shed some of their macabre stereotypes of us. All but the most jingoistic chest-pounders would probably agree that might not be such a bad thing.

***

The spirited conversation with St. Rick and good miles we were making had me in high spirits. *Maybe I've hit a turning point.* But then we reached the turning off point to the Tule Canyon Campsite. By-the-Book was noticeably limping in the opposite direction with some other guy I hadn't seen before.

"What's going on?" I asked.

"I've got a viral blister," he reported. "I have to get off the trail. This gentleman is nice enough to show me a way out of here."

It had to be a coincidence, but my feet had just started throbbing within a couple hundred yards of that. I limped down a hill to what turned out to be an unfortunate campsite. The water was running, but green-colored, and we were completely exposed to the wind. My high spirits of the afternoon flagged. Perhaps Trout Lily had known what she was doing getting the hell out of this campsite and hiking on. Speaking of hell, I was on the verge of my own PCT version of hell.

BILL WALKER

Chapter 11

Renee

"The lesson of history," wrote historian, George Santayana, "is that people *don't* learn the lessons of history."

Adults are just like children in at least one respect. When we put off problems and kick the can down the road, it only gets worse. Much worse. Yet we keep doing it. Maybe it's just the human condition. Perhaps I shouldn't be so hard on myself, though. After all, how many times had I been hiking along and suddenly a knee, shoulder, or foot would inexplicably begin to generate some pain. I might pop some Advil, take a break, whatever. Sometimes, it might even hurt for a day or two. But then, just as inexplicably, it would go away. That was what I had been hoping for here.

But it wasn't happening. On Sunday, May 5, 2009, my feet pretty much were in sharp pain from the beginning. I had blisters on the outside heels of both feet, blisters on one of the toes, and the balls of both feet had a deep burning sensation. That feeling of my feet being inside a furnace (inside two pairs of wool socks and size 14 shoes) had returned. Up until today I had been able to find somewhere—either on the balls, the heels, even on the sides to plant my steps. Now though, this incredibly short-sighted strategy was flashing red alert. I was practically immobilized.

The full wrath of the sun was bearing down on us this day. Every half hour I would stop, take off my socks and shoes, lie down horizontally, and elevate my bare feet on my backpack.

Hikers passed by making various analytical remarks ("so high, so low") about my condition. Finally, I would get up and apply triple-antibiotic ointment, tape them up, and gingerly shuffle off. Twenty or thirty minutes later I'd be laid back low again.

On one of these breaks, a south-bounder from Israel came by.

"Can you hitch from that road coming up?" I quickly asked.

"Yes," he reported. "There's a whole group feeding hikers and giving them rides into town." With that news, I jumped up and frantically began trying to hike using all legs, and as little feet as possible. It slows you down greatly.

"Hector's down there," someone said, referring to the Blister Doctor.

Worried that the group might evaporate, I tried hurrying. But the downhills were especially excruciating. A big group was sitting under the tent watching me limp up pronouncedly. Meadow Mary and her entourage had a big pot of soup, refreshments, and cold beers. Normally, this would have been one of those magic moments that hikers periodically experience where everything is perfect.

Instead, dispensing with all pleasantries, I immediately asked, "Is Hector here?"

"He just left."

"Damn," I flung my hiking pole and backpack down, and lay down under the tent brooding.

***

We hikers have it easy in one respect. There are people that truckle and cater to us like we are the masters of the universe. It is such an overwhelmingly positive experience, that it comes as a real jolt those rare times when we meet someone that is the opposite. And when that person is a doctor it can have serious repercussions for your entire journey.

I say doctor. I couldn't have been more mistaken. The entire town of Idyllwild (population 4,500) didn't have a single doctor for reasons that are mystifying. Dave and I had hitchhiked into town the previous night and gotten a cabin at the rustic Idyllwild

Inn. In one of those quirks of fate, he had idly said, "There's supposed to be a medical clinic near here. I think I'll go have 'em check out my feet."

"Oh, I might pop up there with you," I said.

The person who saw me was a *nurse-practicioner*. In fact, according to rumors I later heard, she was quite the journey-woman nurse-practicioner, having nurse-practicioned all over southern California. I sat there on a patient's table with my shoes and socks off and bandages removed, when an unpleasantly plump woman named Renee barged in.

"Hiker," she barked out, barely suppressing her distaste.

"Yes," I answered, and proceeded to explain. She started going over my feet like a mechanic rifling through a car engine. The look on her face was like somebody had placed a rotten sulfuric egg just under her two nostrils.

"How important is this trip to you?" she suddenly said. *Shouldn't that question be coming later in the appointment?*

"Well, very important," I answered. "I've been planning to hike this trail for years."

"Have you had any blisters or swelling on your face, or anywhere else, recently?" *What the hell is she talking about? This is about my feet.*

"Yeah, I walked all over the beach in Florida in the middle of the day getting ready for this hike," I answered. "My lips swelled up with uh,—I guess—sun blisters really bad for a few days."

"Yeah, well," Renee said with an increasingly sour look on her face, "the way your foot is all swollen up, you may have *herpes of the feet*."

"Herpes of the feet," I repeated in disbelief. *Is there really such a thing?*

"Yeah, and you need to take a good five or ten days off the trail," she said bluntly.

"I'm on a tight schedule," I moaned. "Everybody is hiking together. It's best to stay together in the desert." Boy, I really know who to tell a sob story to, don't I!

"These are awful-looking feet," she said, reaching down

and giving them a quick toss up to make her point. "And look at this left foot. It looks practically gangrenous. See the way this fluid is coming out from these calluses," she pointed out. Sure enough there was fluid leaking out from these calluses. "Those are blisters under the calluses. They could get infected any time. Do you wanna' lose your foot?"

If the ability to confuse and scare the hell out of a patient is the hallmark of a great physician—excuse me, nurse-practicioner—then this lady belonged in the Hall of Fame.

"Well, well, what should I do?" I stammered.

"These blisters need to be debreeded," she

said. "How is that done?" I wondered.

"I have to cut the calluses off to get at the blisters underneath."

"That's gonna' take a long time to get back to where I can hike," I muttered. "Is there any alternative?"

"Well maybe you could try soaking them for a few days and taking antibiotics for the infection. I don't know." She walked straight out before I had a chance to discuss Plan B.

A few minutes later a thirty-ish male walked in with a clipboard.

"We just need you to sign this showing you agree to the procedure and the price," he said.

"But what about the other option—the soaking and the antibiotics?" I asked.

"What other option?" he asked. The communication problems in this clinic seemed to run in all directions. Renee came back in with a determined look about her.

"Lie down on the table." I had no idea what was getting ready to happen. But my feet were badly ravaged, I reasoned. So I laid down on the table.

"Do you fit?" she asked.

"Yes, can't you tell," I fired back with my head and arms draped over the end of the table.

"Oh, these are much worse than I had thought," she immediately said. "I'm going to have to go deep. This might be painful." For the next fifteen minutes I felt like you do at the barbershop, worried the barber is cutting too much, but not sure whether to interrupt.

"Okay, I'm through," she announced.

I pulled up my feet to take a look, and immediately felt sick at my stomach. Seventy percent of my calluses on the balls of my feet were gone. Instead, there was a visible terrace from where calluses ended and the drop down to a deeper red color where she had cut. Yeah, the blisters were gone and in blister heaven. But how the hell was I going to hike to Canada?

Renee commenced wrapping my feet in one layer of surgical tape after another in a way I couldn't possibly hope to replicate. I tensely asked one question after another about the taping, walking, etc. which she robotically answered. Then she was finished.

"You're done for awhile," she said in full-stride as she bolted out of the door.

To be perfectly fair, I was in a helluva' fix when I had hobbled in there this morning. But that was nothing compared to the way I walked out. I could barely make it to the waiting room. After paying I just hung out in the waiting room. Renee came flying through.

"Excuse me, Renee," I said diplomatically. "Could you just give me a ballpark figure of when I should be aiming to get back on the trail again?" She looked at me a couple seconds, as if in thought. Then, she wheeled around and whisked away without saying a word.

"You're done for awhile." Her words rung in my head. She sure showed me.

BILL WALKER

Chapter 12

Bettina

"Is this Renee?" I kept asking.

"Yes, I'm the lady that cut the blisters out of your feet," she said. I was in disbelief.

"Yes, yesterday morning," she assured me. "That was me." I was totally confused.

Dave and I had tried to walk back to the Idyllwild Inn the previous day. But after about twenty yards, he had called the Idyllwild Inn and ask them to come pick me up. They had obliged and I had buried myself back in the cabin for the rest of the day. Deep depression set in. My calculations—entering the high Sierra on June, 15th, getting to Canada before October, etc—all lay in shambles.

Idyllwild was overrun with PCT hikers as the annual wave of thru-hikers was passing through, and word had filtered out about my misfortune. Hikers were dropping by the cabin to commiserate. In reality, though, most simply wanted a firsthand look at the atrocity they had all heard this woman had committed on me.

"I'd call her up and raise hell," Wrongway suggested.

"I'd call her up," Cruiser asserted, "and tell her you were going to sue the shit out of her." Neither fit my laid-back character. However, I did grit my teeth and call the clinic to try to clarify taping instructions. I was braced for a verbal shellacking from Nurse Renee. Surprisingly, they put me right through to her. Much more surprisingly, though, was her attitude. Gone were the surliness and antipathy to hikers. The new Renee was respectful and glad to repeat bandaging and medical instructions over and over to a neurotic ex-patient. Actually, there was even a hint of defensiveness in her speech. Was she remorseful that she had laid me so low? More likely, she was worried because Idyllwild is a small town. And yesterday she had made sure I was going to be here for awhile.

***

Headline: Cougar attacks hiker in the Cleveland National Forest. Dave had turned on the television and this bit of journalistic gold was at the top of the news.

"Hey, isn't the Cleveland National Forest where we are right now?" Dave asked.

"We were," I answered. "I'm not sure if we're still in it." A cougar had attacked a hiker there. The hiker's dog had loyally jumped in to defend the hiker, at which point the cougar had made short work of the dog. The big surprise, though, was that it had occurred in the middle of the day.

"I thought they only moved around at night," Dave said, sounding a bit concerned. He was planning to hike out alone the next morning.

There are about 5,000 cougars in California. They are nocturnal and extremely stealthy. So stealthy that they sometimes follow their victims for days at a time. In fact, most PCT hikers are probably followed by a cougar for awhile, although only about fifteen percent actually see one. They like to hang out on rocks where they spring out to break the back of their prey's necks instantaneously. Fortunately, cougars are such great hunters that they almost always choose tastier prey than us wretched humanoids.

Dave wasn't an alarmist type, but I did notice him watching the local news again that night at 6:00 and 10:00. And when I awoke and went to the bathroom at 3:00 that morning his light was on, and I heard him re-arranging his backpack yet again. He was just retiring in Florida where he had quite a nice lifestyle; this was proving tougher than expected. Off he went alone at first light into one of the most brutal dry stretches in the desert. My heart went out to him.

***

"How tall are you?" came the question from behind me. Never has been my favorite question. But in the literally tens of thousands of times I have fielded it, this would prove to be my very favorite.

I was in the Idyllwild Library, and turned around to see who had asked the question. A sixtyish lady, quite decked out for a public library, stood there smiling at me. Fortunately, I didn't give her one of the sassy answers I occasionally employ. I gave her a straight answer. After all, I was going to be in town awhile.

Every so often in trail towns you meet that rare person who is ga-ga over us smelly tramps. That was the case here with this woman, named *Bettina*. I was with Just Jack, who had very thoughtfully come by that morning and offered to carry my backpack to the Idyllwild campground, where I was now planning to stay the rest of my convalescence. But all I could think about was how difficult it was going to be to keep my wounded feet clean and properly bandaged at the campground.

"How would you two guys like to come up to my place for dinner and a drink?" Bettina asked.

No brainer. "Yes." Let me say right off the bat, I had more than a drink in mind. But, it might not be what you think.

We got in her Cadillac and she drove up a steep hill to a picturesque chalet (the smallest of her three houses), which was two streets down from Dolly Parton's vacation home.

"Has everybody in Idyllwild learned to stare at the pavement when Dolly walks by?" I asked.

"No," Bettina answered. "She gets mad when people don't come up and greet her."

Bettina opened her house up to us like long-lost relatives, and we sipped drinks on her veranda which had a majestic view overlooking the mountains.

I'm usually shy in these matters and operate through indirection. But this time was different; I was in a pickle. So I popped the question directly to Bettina.

"Bettina," I asked. "Is there any way in the world I could sleep a few nights out here on this veranda?"

"Honey," she answered, "I've got a whole second floor with two bedrooms empty. You can stay there until you learn to walk again." Better yet, with Just Jack I had a witness to the great trail magic I had just scored. Hikers love swapping stories about what they've scored in trail towns. I had just scored a luxurious mountain chalet to recuperate. But Jack had greater ambitions than being a mere witness.

All I can say is that it's honest-to-God a shame that his feelings weren't fully reciprocated by Bettina. He sure as heck would have been a step up from her three previous husbands. I know because I would hear one vehement monologue after another about all of them in the next two weeks at her house. Instead of making common cause with Jack though, Bettina took a strange shine to me. And it would play itself out in bizarre ways over the next couple weeks.

You could have reasonably assumed I was Nurse Renee's biggest critic in Idyllwild. Not by a long shot. Bettina was.

"She almost cut a friend's finger off, I swear to God. She's worked for every medical clinic in southern California and keeps getting fired. She'll be gone from here by the end of the year." And on and on, day after day. It was depressing. But her tirades weren't limited to Renee, either. I had chatted with a much older, much heavier woman in a restaurant the night I had hobbled into Idyllwild. Her name was Teva.

"I know everybody in Idyllwild," Bettina repeatedly said.

"Do you know an older lady named Teva?" I had asked her and described Teva. It probably wasn't a great description because I only met her that once for about five minutes and never saw her again. That last fact didn't register with Bettina, however. Any time I went into town after that she would question me obsessively after returning about whether I had seen Teva.

Another lady in town who puts up hikers came to Bettina's house to bring me some get-well cake. The lady could barely make it up the steps to the veranda because she had gained 85 pounds in one year. But that didn't stop Bettina from getting paranoid about her.

"Sky, when is your friend going to bring you some more cake," she kept chiding me. "You miss her, don't you?"

***

"Renee, this is Bettina McAllister," Bettina said. I couldn't believe my ears. *Renee.*

"I'm with Skywalker," Bettina continued on her cell phone. "We all think you owe Skywalker a look at his feet."

Bettina paused for a comment on the other end and then answered, "Right now in Iberico Restaurant."

We were in the finest restaurant in Idyllwild, which happened to be about the only place Bettina ever ate. Bettina had convinced the couple, Ron and Dana, whom we were eating with (who were actually friends of Renee's) to give her Renee's home phone number. Mega-blunder. Fifteen minutes later Renee arrived in the restaurant. It was a weeknight about 9 o' clock so she had been working all day. She stood right in front of our table, uncomfortably shifting weight from one leg to another.

"Well," she asked sheepishly, "what does everybody want me to do—look at his feet?" Ron, Dana, and Bettina nodded gravely. When I started taking off my shoes the waiter saw what was going on and rushed up.

"Sir, could you please do this away from all our other guests?" he asked. Renee and I dutifully went to an empty table where I put my feet up on the table cloth. But that had the waiter rushing over again pleading, "Please, please, keep your feet off the table."

"They look a little better," Renee said quietly. "Keep soaking them and airing them out." She again sounded defensive. It was pretty clear there were *two* people in Idyllwild that were very worried about my feet. But for very different reasons.

We walked back to the table, where I sat down and Renee remained standing. But Bettina, who was not feeling the least bit of pain by this point, wasn't going to let Renee's long day end.

"You don't belong in Idyllwild," she loudly said to Renee. Renee froze, which allowed Bettina to sucker-punch her some more.

"You've been fired," Bettina continued, "from at least two health clinics I know in Long Beach and Santa Barbara." Ron and Dana were listening to this in disbelief. We all wanted to crawl under the table. Finally, Renee struck back.

"I haven't got to take this," she fired at the whole table.

She turned to me, "You're going around telling all the hikers I screwed your feet up." I didn't offer any protest because her charge was true. I had been.

"People on the Appalachian Trail start off hiking nine miles a day and work themselves in. But here everybody starts trying to do twenty miles a day from the beginning. Then they all get to Idyllwild and come to my office wondering why their feet are all screwed up."

She continued, "I don't care what you tell the hikers. But I don't want some drunk lady spreading lies here in Idyllwild that hurt my reputation." She then turned to reprimand her friends Ron and Dana. "Please don't be giving out my phone number to any more drunks." More silence from our table.

"I've gotta' work tomorrow," she said to herself, as much as any of us. With that she turned and off she went. The entire restaurant had gone silent over the whole drama.

The whole thing reminded me a little bit of Captain Queeg in *The Caine Mutiny*. He had started off looking like a nutty character in charge of the ship. But as the extent of his challenges became more clear, he began to look a little more sympathetic (In fact, a few months after I was in Idyllwild, Renee was fired. That same week her daughter hung herself from a tree outside town).

***

I became desperate to get out of Idyllwild. My feet were slowly getting better. But it would have been suicidal to go out in the desert and try hiking on them just yet. I started hitchhiking into town every morning. There I would hang out on a shaded bench in front of the post office and let my feet air out.

Meanwhile, I had new pairs of shoes coming in from all over

the country. I would pick up a pair practically every morning at the post office. But none of them seemed suitable for desert hiking, and I sent them all back. Repeatedly, I checked the REI website to see if Vasque had any size 15's. Forget it. *What in the world am I going to do?*

Several people had counseled me to just take my Vasque 14's and cut the front out of them to allow my feet some breathing room. Many hikers performed such surgery on their shoes, and I was tentatively planning to do it myself. Then, I idly typed in Vasque Size 15 into the Google search box. I couldn't believe my eyes. Right there a list of Vasque Size 15's came up, including the exact brand I wanted, from *Dick's Sporting Goods*. I had them over-nighted to Idyllwild and my shoe problems for the next 2,500 miles were now solved. But what an excruciating price I had paid for my lack of due diligence.

The whole bubble of thru-hikers had already passed through Idyllwild. I would now be hiking alone in the desert.

Chapter 13

Comeback

Of all the kinds of silences—the stillness of snowfields—none is as total as the desert. It is the hush of antiquity.

The High Adventure of Eric Ryback

The silence was deafening. It was the middle of the day with the temperature well over 100 degrees. My foot, while not completely healed, actually felt pretty good for "regular" life. The calluses wouldn't be completely grown back for another few weeks. But it was only going to get hotter in the desert. So I had heavily taped up my feet, packed up my backpack, popped some Advil, and hitched back to the trailhead after seventeen days in Idyllwild.

To the left, right, straight ahead, and behind was a scene of monolithic desert—brown, sandy dune hills with chaparral bushes. The austere landscape matched my mood.

Jack London had vividly written about the Alaskan Yukon:

A vast silence reigned over the land. There was a hint in it of laughter, but a laughter more terrible than any sadness. It was the masterful wisdom of eternity laughing at the futility of life.

Timeless desert scene

The Alaskan back country and the desert, of course, couldn't be more different. But they did have one thing in common. They were inhospitable to humanity to the point of downright mocking us. I wasn't scared, but rather in a sort of low-grade depression. At times like this you have only yourself to fall back on, and it's best to stick to fundamentals. I concentrated on taking measured, cautious steps in my new Vasque Size 15 trail shoes. They were big to be sure, but I was wearing two pairs of wool socks (hikers should never, ever wear cotton) to help fill them up and cushion the impact on my feet.

In some basic ways this was a purer than normal outdoor experience for me. I had no idea how far I was going to go today, where I was going to camp, and no expectations of any human encounters. I was just going to follow this 2 ½ foot-wide trail through the desert and take what comes. On my back were about 45 pounds, including a week's supply of food and five liters (almost 11 pounds) of water, the most I'd ever carried. Every time I heard the water sloshing around in my bottles, it reminded me they were my lifeline.

I quickly became winded and had to take frequent breaks.

At first I thought it was from the layoff, but actually the trail was climbing up to 7,000 feet and high desert. With nobody to chat with, I kept the breaks short. By dark I had done about 15 miles, set up camp, and felt like a PCT hiker again.

Unfortunately, when I got in my tent and removed all the tape and bandages from my feet, they were covered in black dirt. Further, the filth didn't just cover the bandages, but reached under where the calluses had been. *Infection.* That was my greatest fear. I decided to use some of the precious water I had been carrying to try to clean the open wounds off. But it would be impossible to prevent it from happening again the next day in the grimy desert.

***

Thru-hikers are renowned for breaking camp in the morning at breakneck speed. But now I had to carefully administer ointment, pads, and surgical tape to each foot in my tent before breaking camp. The balls of my feet where Renee had cut deepest were throbbing. That was bad news because day two is the key day when coming back from an injury.

I focused on making every single step with as little pain as possible. Needless to say, that is a losing proposition. While rock-hopping on my heels across Holcomb Creek, I bought it— *splash*— straight into the drink. After quickly pulling myself out of the stream I thought, *Hey, try to turn this into a positive.* So I decided to take an extended break right there to soak my feet in this rare desert stream, hoping to numb them. However, the bees were utterly ferocious in the shade where I leaned on a rock. That was another dilemma of desert hiking. On your breaks you had a choice between roasting in the broiling sun or let the bees molest you in the shade. It was positively hellish.

***

Struggle is one thing. Damaging your physical self is another. And that's what I was doing. I needed to get out of here. But I had no idea how. So I fell back on the automatic default position.

When in doubt a hiker hikes. We are creatures with great

faith that if we just continue moving forward, somehow, something good will happen. My steps were stiff and clodding, with heavy emphasis on the heels. I was lucky to make a mile at a time before having to take a break. While reclining glumly up against my backpack I heard the first voices in a couple days coming from the opposite direction. It was a couple carrying daypacks. Immediately, the old hiker *Yogi-ing* instincts surged to the forefront.

"Excuse me," I said to this pleasant-looking middle-aged couple, "Could you tell me if there happen to be any roads or any towns around here at all?"

"Well, yes," the man said. "Where are you trying to get to?"

I didn't want to overplay my hand too quickly. First, I had to cajole them into letting me into their car. They described a complex series of dirt roads, turning into paved roads, into other paved roads.

"Is there any way in the world you could give me a lift up to that first paved road?" I earnestly asked.

"Sure, sure, we'd be glad to drop you off up there," he said.

Slowly, but surely, I drew snake eyes with this couple. He was a preacher at some remote hamlet called Mount Gregory. After I began talking rhapsodically about the wonders of the PCT, he suddenly said to his wife, "Honey, we haven't been to Big Bear Lake in awhile. Would you like to have dinner there tonight?"

They drove me 1 ½ hours south on a winding mountain road, and dropped me at Big Bear Lake Hostel.

***

Deep down I knew I had to do it. In fact, I had known it for some time. The three-day comeback hike had been almost *proforma*—to prove to myself that there was no alternative. I was going to have to skip forward. I had hiked every blaze of the Appalachian Trail and dearly wanted to hike every step of the Pacific Crest Trail. This was supposed to be my hike-to-end-all- long-hikes. Now it wouldn't be pure.

My mother and brother consoled me with phone calls. "Bill, that's great you take such pride in the whole thing," my mother reasoned. "But does it really matter to anyone else whether you do the entire trail or not?"

Sounds reasonable, to be sure. Was there an egocentric element to thru-hiking? Probably, and to that extent it is not a terribly worthy endeavor. But there was another big issue.

Knowing you have a long journey to complete forces you to keep hiking on low morale days, if the weather is crummy, or maybe you feel like lingering in a trail town. It was a great motivating force. Now that I would no longer be a virgin, would I be able to muster that same sustained effort?

Fortunately, I was able to catch a ride to the one place more than any other that exudes the spirit of the PCT. Suddenly, I was surrounded by swarms of hikers and couldn't have been happier about it.

BILL WALKER

Chapter 14

Donna

You know—if we males just didn't have such damn egos, we'd be alright. I stood there with another male hiker with yet another male ego taking in the whole scene at the Saufleys.

It was a brilliant tapestry. You couldn't help noticing the number of truly fine-feathered females flitting around all over the place. They were loving the attention and having the time of their lives.

"What are these girls," this guy commented to me, "cheerleaders or hikers?"

"Yeah," I said light-heartedly, trying to make conversation. "I bet some of 'em don't even have backpacks and are just trying to act like they're hikers."

I said ego, right? You're welcome to label us with stronger adjectives.

In any event, the girls were damn good-looking and having a damn good time. This guy and I also were proven to be dead-wrong. The next morning I noticed some very noticeable girls packing up their backpacks and preparing to head off, while the guys were taking their seats in a circle of chairs. Among the girls leaving was Luna, who we would all see a lot more of. She had just given a guy a Mohawk haircut to great applause, at which point she proceeded to head off alone into the desert.

She was soon followed by the dynamic duo of Root Canal and Color Blind. I looked at the physiques of those two and thought, "I'd be lucky to keep up with them for even a day." Male hikers soon started calling Root Canal by a different name—Turbo Puss. Guess which name stuck?

Again, I wish we weren't such pigs. Maybe this Chinese-style confession will make me less so.

***

The best place for a hiker hostel is in the middle of nowhere. By that measure, the Saufleys in Agua Dulce are perfectly located. Their hostel, *Hiker Haven*, lies slap-dab in the middle of perhaps the most featureless part of the entire southern California desert.

Hiker morale is often low upon arrival. And once you arrive on the main street in Agua Dulce there ain't a helluva' lot in the way of civilization, including no motels. Into this vacuum steps the strong, determined personality of Donna Saufley.

Immediately, Donna reminded me of Nancy Pelosi, only minus twenty years and a half-million dollars in cosmetic surgery. The similarities were not just in physical appearance, but also in style. Pelosi is renowned for running the U.S. House of Representatives with an iron fist; but cross her at your own risk. Donna was nowhere near so ruthless. But it was very clear from the beginning that you were a guest at her house and to play by her rules. Fortunately, she was determined, seemingly to the point of obsession, to make it a pleasant stay.

Every year she orders fifty cots to be set up under huge tarps in her backyard, along with two RV's. One of the RV's is outfitted with computers, kitchen facilities, and a shower (sign up on the wall), all operating on a backup generator she has installed. Because Agua Dulce has no post office she has turned her garage into a state-of-the art system for handling the many packages of food, shoes, equipment, maps, etc. Multiple washing machines and dryers are in constant use. Rather than a nightly charge, donations are into a jar on the honor system. All I can say is that I hope like heck she and her husband break even, because the expense is considerable.

The maximum stay is two nights, unless injured. It quickly became clear this rule was a necessary evil. Hikers get very comfortable here after 100 grueling miles through the desert, and don't want to be thrust right back into the oven so soon. She regularly has to shush people on out of here, and back into the desert.

I didn't fit in any of the available bunks, which visibly bothered Donna.

"Skywalker, set your tent up right here," pointing to a plot of grass right in front of her house. The second night she found me an extra-long cot under one of the tents that, to my great surprise, I fit in.

The hiker box (where hikers throw away excess or dysfunctional gear) at the Saufleys blew my mind. Mountains of shoes, some of them looking like they had been worn just a few times, were stacked up in a huge box. The box just for New Balance shoes, the most widely worn brand on the trail, was especially bulging. Obviously, the desert had been hell on a lot more than just my feet.

Donna knew that. They immediately had me soaking my feet in a machine full of hot salt water. She also allowed me to stay an extra night, which you had to justify. She was determined that her place would be about getting you ready to hike—not partying. Unfortunately, others had some different ideas.

***

"Where did they all go?" Donna asked in surprise.

"They're all doing the 24 beer thing," somebody answered.

"What 24 beer thing?" Donna asked sharply.

"You know—the tradition where everybody drinks the 24 beers in 24 miles."

"No, I don't know about any 24 beer tradition," Donna said, sounding alarmed.

A group of raging alpha males had been sitting around a circle that day drinking beers; someone had dreamt up the fantasy that PCT hikers traditionally try to drink 24 beers in the 24 mile stretch from the Saufleys to the legendary Anderson's hostel.

"Chopper and Savior aren't in that group, are they?" Donna quickly asked.

"Yes, they are," somebody answered.

"I can't believe it," Donna visibly cringed.

I soon learned that Chopper and Savior's mother had died several years ago in that exact section they were now hiking. She had gotten lost and died from hypothermia. Now her two accident-prone sons were attempting to drink 24 beers each, in the section where she had perished. Perhaps Donna had reason to worry.

***

"Skywalker, Skywalker, hey, which one is Skywalker?"

"Here I am."

It was 4 o'clock in the morning, and it was a bit alarming to be awakened in such a frantic way. The previous night I had chatted extensively to an African-American former Special-Forces soldier named Pete. Between the cold fog that had blown in and the ample quantities of alcohol he had consumed, he couldn't find me in the sea of cots.

"Where's the trail go out of here?" Pete asked hurriedly. After groggily giving him a basic route, I asked, "You're not going now, are you?"

"Yeah, I've got to catch up with those other guys."

"Wait til' morning and I'll go with you," I said.

"I've gotta' go now," Pete said, and hurried off in the thick fog.

However, it wasn't to be the last I saw of him today. A few hours later, a car pulled up to the Saufleys. None other than Pete emerged, with blood pouring from his knee.

"What happened?"

"Got hit by a car," Pete said matter-of-factly.

Donna immediately took over and had him icing his knee and a doctor's appointment.

"Who did it?" someone asked him.

"Oh, it was just a bunch of kids," he said offhandedly. "They didn't see me. It's all good, no worries."

Pete's calmness in this crucible earned him the trail name, *No Pain*.

No Pain then sat there regaling us with stories of his days

in Special Ops, tumbling out of airplanes, drinking urine, you name it. He was also a veteran Appalachian Trail hiker.

"Last December, I'm in my tent in Shenandoah National Park eating a pizza," he recounted. "A male bear comes busting in there— you know males don't hibernate in the winter the way females do. The bear threw my ass right out of my tent and ate my pizza."

To nobody's surprise, No Pain was soon back on the trail.

Chapter 15

The Andersons

Amazingly, after all the people at the Saufleys, I again found myself alone in the desert. Immediately, I got lost near some power lines and walked up a hill before noticing the footprints I had been following had given out. I scurried around worriedly, before spotting a familiar oval-shaped PCT sign down the hill to the left. God knows what would have happened if I had been hiking drunk at night like that group last night.

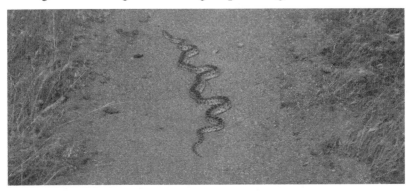

Rattlesnakes are fish-in-water in the desert;
you couldn't say the same about hikers.

While I didn't come across many humans, I did see plenty that I wasn't terribly keen to see. I turned a corner and there traveled a rattler, sloping off the trail. Twenty yards later another one lay coiled up in the middle of the trail. Immediately, I backed up, making sure I wasn't getting too near the previous one. Then, I just ran around the coiled snake which remained lying there in the middle of the trail. There was no sudden uncoiling of a serpent like in Greek mythology.

Like every hiker, I was trying to develop a better idea in my mind of the most likely places *where* you'd spot rattlesnakes. I never was able to develop a reliable profile, but there was a clear pattern as to *when* I saw them. It almost always was late in the afternoon after the worst heat of the day. This, not coincidentally, is when hikers are most active.

***

I was absolutely rocked; it was possibly the most unbelievable site I ever have seen, and maybe ever will see.

It had been a pretty 'good foot day'—maybe a seven out of ten. My simple focus had been on the water cache at mile 18 for the day.

I turned a bend in the trail and in a clump of bushes to the left was the desert version of a haunted house. *The Andersons.* They had hung goblins and skeletons in all the bushes. Better yet, they had stashed plentiful gallons of water.

I scanned the area for 200 yards in both directions looking for suitable campsites. Unfortunately, the only place my two-person tent would fit was right in the middle of the PCT. So I had waited until right before dark to erect it. Of course, cougars wander around all over at night, including occasionally on the trail. But I had the thin membrane of my tent to protect me from any misunderstanding with them.

In the middle of the night, I got out of my tent to urinate. When I happened to look up at the sky, I was suddenly seized. The stars shined in a bolder, clearer fashion than I could have ever imagined. It honestly felt as though I was scanning the wide-arc of the heavens with a powerful telescope. Like humans in desert settings through the ages, I felt stirred to my greatest depths.

***

It was Sunday morning, and everybody looked pretty much gone already. No, not as in gone to church. They were gone as in drunk. And they were just getting started.

"I'm not going to stay here for long," was my first reaction.

I'd hitchhiked into Green Valley, California, site of the PCT-famous hostel, Casa de Luna.

"Skywalker, get a shirt on," several hikers, looking like Turkish sultans, encouraged me.

Over to the side was a big rack of Hawaiian shirts. Most of the dozen-or-so hikers sitting here had arrived knee-walking drunk yesterday morning, including five of them who had successfully completed the 24 beer challenge. Needless to say, they were retelling the whole story for the umpteenth time. Soon a middle-aged woman emerged from the house.

"Welcome, I'm Terrie," she introduced herself. "I hear you've got a foot injury. She immediately set me up soaking my feet in salt water.

As we sat there chatting, somebody suddenly yelled, "Terrie, here he comes!"

I looked over and saw a police car slowly passing right by their driveway. In what was obviously a well-honed routine, Terrie quickly placed her cigarette in her mouth, dropped her drawers, and revealed her ample rear-end right at the policeman. I say policeman; he was really a police boy—all of probably about 23, but looked 18. He looked like a little kid stealing a glance at a Playboy Magazine, he was so saucer-eyed. I soon noticed he rode by several times a day; he was probably new and that earned him the assignment from headquarters to keep his eye on this place, *Casa de Luna.*

***

The counter-culture element on any hiking trail is bound to be strong. Normally, however, it was integrated with the more *de rigueur* aspects of hiking. Here, though, it was on full display. I had been too young for Woodstock and the Age of Aquarius, so I reckon this was the closest I'd ever get to it.

Romances were struck up in this free-for-all atmosphere. One free-spirited hiker with a striking resemblance to the 1960's musician, *Tiny Tim*, became interested in a Canadian hiker named Josephine. He was not only successful, but other hikers gushed for hundreds of miles at his effortless style in winning over this shapely girl. Another guy, Five Dollar, who was a Mormon (although you would never know it) began an incendiary relationship with a girl named *Not a Chance*. This was impressive for the simple reason she had previously rebuffed other chatty male hikers with the memorable words, "Not a Chance."

One group of hikers packed up their backpacks every morning to head back to the trail. However, after eating the pancakes Joe Anderson cooked for everybody, somebody would always crack a beer, followed by the sounds of other beer cans being opened. The kiss of death was sitting in the black sofa that everybody labeled *the vortex*. The manager, Doug, who is the single most laid-back human I've ever had the privilege to meet and who has yet to ever be seen in public without a beer in his hand, would laugh at them and say, "You're not going anywhere." He was almost always right.

By late afternoon, they would make their last lame statement, "I'm leaving after taco salad tonight."

Finally, after the trail-famous taco salad dinner and a few more beers, they would hoist their backpacks and head back to the *Magical Forest* (the Anderson's backyard) to cowboy camp.

Honestly though, several hikers never seemed to recover psychologically from the whole experience. To them, *this* was the summit of the PCT, not Mount Whitney or Forrester Pass in the Sierras, or Manning Park in Canada. Every future trail town was a letdown to them after the Andersons. They talked about it repeatedly hereafter. Some even suspiciously got lost in the desert after leaving here and called Joe and Terrie to come pick them back up.

Joe and Terrie Anderson, themselves, have a miraculous, unequivocal love for smelly hikers, and their hostel is one of the worthwhile attractions of the PCT. Honest-to-God, I never felt so welcome anywhere besides home.

Chapter 16

The Mojave Desert

The Mojave is the most sterile and repulsive
desert I have ever seen.

John C. Fremont

You can meet the damndest people in the desert. By that same line of reasoning, the Mojave should have the damndest people of all. But you had better know how to get along with them. They can play key roles.

A 47-mile dry stretch on the PCT is broken up by one lone redoubt that hikers pass by. It is at a place called *Desert Bazaar*, and is also the official entry point into the Mojave Desert. I wandered up to Desert Bazaar alone in the middle of the afternoon wondering what I had just stumbled on. What greeted me was a scene out of the Wild, Wild West, including the façade of a saloon, jail, post office, and library. *What is all this?*

When I saw the garage was open, I wandered in there to seek refuge from the bullying wind. Here, I met the strangest person on the entire PCT.

"What are you at my house for?" came the question rifled at me.

"Uh, well," I stammered, "I was hoping to stay here tonight before heading off into the Mojave tomorrow."

"Where are you going to stay?" he fired back.

"I see the RV's," I answered, "but it doesn't look like I fit in the beds."

"Why didn't you tell me? I've got a long bed in the jail,"

"Oh, yeah. Is there anybody in there?"

"Yeah," he said, "some drunk has been staying in there, but I'm tired of feeding him. Tell him he can get going."

"Do I need a key?"

"No, go on in there."

I wandered straight over into the building marked JAIL. When I looked inside the bars there was a child-sized bed with a doll in it. Score one for the owner over naïve me.

When I got back in the garage, some cooked pasta was waiting. "You want some pasta?" he asked sharply. "Yeah, that would be great," I answered.

"Give me some money," he held out his hand.

We got that straightened out and he then offered me a bucket and salt water for soaking my feet. As I sat there eating pasta and soaking my feet I thought, *this guy's not so bad*. But that's when he moved in for the kill.

"You know the problem with hikers," he barked at me.

"Where would I even begin," I countered.

"They don't share their women," he responded with great certitude. "There were two couples that had both of my RV's rocking all night last night. And you'll never believe what they did."

"What?" I wondered.

"They never invited me in there to participate."

The *gentleman* with whom I was interlocuting was the owner, Richard Tatum. He was in his mid-sixties and a spitting image of the comedian, Don Rickles. But Rickles had always seemed to have a rational side to him. The fellow in front of me appeared stark mad.

"The one thing I can't stand though," Richard said, "is when people don't give me the respect I deserve. Nobody disses *Big Dick*."

"You hear what I'm saying?" he asked. "Do you understand?"

"Yeah," I said mildly, wondering where this was going.

"I'm Big Dick," Richard shouted. "Do you believe me?"

"Yes," I answered.

"Let me show you," he said, unzipping his pants.

"That's okay," I quickly said.

"Take a look at Big Dick."

"No," I pleaded.

I jerked my head away just a split-second before Big Dick could directly display his badge of manhood to me. Close call.

Quickly, I decided a better place to seek refuge from the stiff wind was outside of the garage behind a car. *Left Field* soon walked up with that expectant look hikers adopt after being out in the desert for a few days.

"Hey Skywalker," he said, "what are you doing sitting here?"

"Just getting everything straight in my backpack for tomorrow."

"Is the owner in there?"

Left Field and I had maintained a running verbal battle for a good while now, which we both enjoyed. He was only 21 years old, but his every move bespoke, "I'm in command of things."

I decided this was a good time to test his mettle.

"Sure, go check in with him," I responded, but gave him no heads-up of what to expect.

Ten minutes later he walked out and looked at me with a mixture of amusement and shock.

"Is it just me," he asked, "or is this guy batshit crazy?"

We laughed in unison as he kept looking at me for a specific response.

"Did he, uh?" I began to ask.

"Yeah," he nodded with his face flushed.

Left Field had finally met his match in Big Dick.

Fortunately, we were to see that there was a lot more to Big Dick than his initial raffish behavior. Without this lonely, windswept outpost to provide some relief, traversing the Mojave would be quite a bit more complicated for a PCT hiker. Given the overall harshness, it's not surprising that quite the mercurial character is the Mojave's gatekeeper.

***

"The Mojave Desert offers a blend of splendor, stark beauty, and vast expanses not found anywhere else in the country," wrote the *Defenders of Wildlife*. All I can say is it takes an especially romantic person or organization to have such a love-love relationship with the Mojave Desert.

Nonetheless, millions of Americans have chosen to live here. Las Vegas, with a population of nearly two million, is the largest city in the Mojave; almost a million people in the eastern Los Angeles metropolitan area live within the boundaries of the Mojave as well. Millions more flock annually to see the Badwater Basin in Death Valley National Park, the lowest point in the entire United States (-282 feet).

Temperatures in the same place can easily vary 80 degrees in one day. Readings below zero degrees are common in the winter, but in the summer temperatures can easily exceed 130 degrees. Annual rainfall is usually less than five inches. The environment is simply inhospitable to human life, except in those oases created by modern irrigation techniques. Heck, it's even harsh to animals judging by how few you see out there. And the ones you see are almost all poisonous.

***

I was very reluctant to go out in the Mojave alone for fear of getting lost. Left Field had fled immediately after yesterday's incident, and everybody was scattered.

Fortunately, a foursome had hiked into Desert Bazaar at dark the previous evening. I had seen them before at the Saufleys and the Andersons, and they appeared to be that rare thing—a close knit foursome. Unlike most groups, they appeared to have what it took to stick together. For starters, there were two guys and two girls.

The males, *Dirk* and *Snake Charmer*, were both west-coasters in their late thirties. The two girls, *Laura*, a charming mid-thirtyish lady from London, and Ingrid a tall, graceful German girl in her late twenties, were both plenty attractive. No matter what somebody might try to tell you, that helps maintain group unity. I sound like I know what I'm talking about on this topic which, of course, I don't. But in this case the results speaks for themselves. They'd been together since the Kickoff, despite having very different hiking styles and speeds.

They had been so sequestered, in fact, that I was even reluctant to broach the subject of hiking out with them this morning. Finally, I just started walking along into the Mojave with them. I was soon glad I had.

We arrived at a confusing maze of dirt roads that all looked the same. A group the previous day had missed a turn here and ended up twenty miles off course (Perhaps not so coincidentally, it was the same group that had Big Dick so stoked up about rocking his RV's the previous night). Fortunately, one of the German girl Ingrid's many talents was map reading, and she figured out which direction we should head.

The Mojave is basically a desert floor and utterly featureless. For mile after mile we walked in an arrestingly ugly landscape. For the most part, it was the easiest possible place to hike, despite hikers carrying up to 7 liters (15 pounds) of water. Some people had been talking for weeks about night-hiking all the way through it. However, a heavy cloud cover was to hold the entire time we were in the Mojave. Instead of burning up, I struggled to stay warm.

The sole aesthetically appealing feature I could notice was the Joshua trees (named by the early Mormon settlers after the prophet, Joshua). These sturdy green trees with sharp, spindly branches are indigenous to the Mojave and often marks its boundaries.

The only human construction in this entire milieu may have been the ugliest thing of all. I refer to the closed aqueduct piping system that runs for 223 miles through the desert. It contains the water supply for the city of Los Angeles. Quite a story lies behind it.

***

A long-living urban legend has it that Los Angeles stole its water. That is not true. Technically, it's not anyway. The city stayed within legal bounds at all times. But make no mistake—through secrecy, guile, subterfuge, and all the rest, the city pulled off something akin to the world's second oldest profession in pursuit of the I.

In the late 19th century, San Francisco was the closest thing the United States had to sophisticated European splendor. Los Angeles was far behind and chafed at its second-class status. Its population had finally begun catching up, though. In fact, L.A.'s population was doubling every five years. However, future growth of the city faced one huge roadblock—lack of water.

The fundamental problem was that most of the water in California lies in the northern part of the state. The massive amounts of precipitation off the Pacific Ocean collide with the western slopes of the Sierras. It's not uncommon to have 100 inches of snow on one side of the mountains and less than ten inches only fifty miles away. San Francisco, but not Los Angeles, has easy access to most of these swollen rivers flowing to their Pacific outlets.

Unfortunately, on the eastern side of the mountains, the few rivers that flow are usually much less substantial. There is one exception. Let me rephrase that; there *was* one exception—the Owens River.

Just south of Yosemite, there is a break in the Sierra chain. The monstrous snowfalls that normally collide with the western banks of the Sierras come barreling through this gunshot pass, creating a rushing river flowing south through the Owens Valley. The lake into which the river empties—or, I should say, used to empty—was Owens Lake. It receives enough water from the Owens River to satiate the daily water needs of 2 million people.

The problem for Los Angeles was how to drain a lake 250 miles away from its city limits. The answer is that Owens Lake lay at 4,000 feet, while Los Angeles sits at almost sea level. Therefore, it was physically possible, even a century ago, for Los Angeles to move that water from the mountains to the city.

First, though, Los Angeles needed to acquire the rights to

the water in the Owens Valley. The story, entertainingly told in Marc Reisner's *Desert Cadillac*, is a lot like you might expect—one of high-minded vision, intermingled with greed, chicanery, exploitation, and con men. A few Los Angeles officials plotted in secrecy and conspired with a double-agent in the Owens Valley to buy up all its land. The ranchers who sold out their land consoled themselves that the Owens River was a generous enough desert river to satiate the needs of 2,000,000 people. *Los Angeles would never be that big.*

The rest, as they say, is history. Los Angeles built a 223 mile aqueduct from the Owens Lake to the city of Los Angeles. No city or country had ever built anything so large across such merciless terrain. Their obsession with getting their hands on this prize was such that they did it all with city money, maintaining a work force of several thousand on the city payroll. They came in under budget and finished it in six years.

This water has allowed Los Angeles to become the second largest desert city in the world, just behind Cairo, Egypt on the Nile. But, of course, Los Angeles has now grown to multiples larger than the two million people that the Owens River can satisfy. They have since built an aqueduct draining water out of the Colorado River—a project that practically led to civil war with the state of Arizona. This was billed as the final solution to Los Angeles' water problem. Of course, it wasn't. They have also had to go into other rivers in northern California and southern Oregon to divert water. They now speak of trying to divert water from as far away as Alaska's Yukon River.

Water is, and will remain, an obsession here in the West. If I was from Canada, which is the Saudi Arabia of water, sharing a long border with such a water-thirsty colossus might just make me a little uneasy. Just as the 20th century was all too often the era of petro-conflict, the 21st century may be the age of *aqua-conflict.*

***

Finally, the PCT diverted away from the monotony of the Los Angeles aqueduct piping. For the first time since arriving at the Mexican border, I even felt a few drops of rain. *What do you do when it rains in the desert?* Desert rainstorms usually only last about ten minutes, but during that time you can expect to be lashed.

We arrived at our intended destination, the Cottonwood Creek Bridge. The water was flowing, which gave me a sigh of relief. Had it not been, I might have had to turn around tomorrow and backtrack all the way to the faucet outside Big Dick's garage. Given this particular prospect, let me say it again—I was relieved to see the water was flowing.

The foursome I was with was not of the free-flowing campsite conversation ilk. Rather, they set their tents up right next to each other, and quickly buried themselves inside.

"What, do ya'll miss Richard or something?" I yelled at them ensconced in their tents.

"Speak for yourself," Laura corrected me.

Of course, it was raining so maybe it just showed they had a little bit more sense than somebody like me who wanted to sit out in the rain yakking about the day's hike.

***

To my great surprise, the British girl, Laura, burst away like a rocket the next morning, looking like a runaway slave fleeing from the master's dogs. Perhaps her soft British accent and effeminate mannerisms had fooled me. Actually, though, I found Laura's speed somewhat instructive. She was about 5'4", and didn't appear very athletic. But if you looked closely at her (which, of course, I assiduously did), she was solidly built in the mid-section. That's where your speed comes from. Dirk, who was only about 5'7", was the only one who could keep up with her. The two trailing hikers were the lanky ones, myself and Ingrid.

Ingrid was an interesting case study. She had just completed a doctorate in English Linguistics, and was interviewing for college professorships. In fact, just since beginning the trail, she had traveled back to Germany to accept an academic award. She was more than just a European intellectual, though. During college, she had worked as a back-country ranger one season in Olympic National Park in Washington State. In a deliberate German way, she did everything by the book—continually followed her maps, hung her food at campsites, bathed in streams, and ate better than any other hiker out here. In fact, she needed two different food bags to hold all the nutritious foods she routinely bought. She also routinely carried two weighty tomes for nighttime reading in her tent, which made her backpack bulging heavy.

Her backpack wasn't as heavy as it could have been, however. The reason was that *Dirk* was carrying one of her two food bags in his backpack. This had generated the predictable winks and nods amongst other hikers, to be sure. But hiking along with them, I quickly saw it wasn't the Faustian bargain that some had hypothesized.

Best-selling novelist, Nelson DeMille, wrote in the *The Gatehouse:*

> When women and men are friends, there's almost always a sexual element present. Not romantic sex, perhaps, but a sort of Freudian concept of sex that acknowledges the attraction as more than platonic, but not quite rising to the level of 'let's screw'.

Dirk was obviously not immune to the charms of having a European girl with a bit of glamor as his steady hiking partner. Nonetheless, he admirably steeled himself several times a day to mention "my girlfriend", referring to a woman back at his home in Washington.

The fourth person in this group was Snake Charmer, who had picked up his name when a rattlesnake had lunged at him in the early days in the desert. Snake Charmer had this horrible crush on Laura. I say horrible—what was wrong with it at all? For starters, he was following a centuries-long tradition of American males and females swooning over our more articulate, and polished British cousins (at least until we get to know them a little better!). In fact, *guess who* was a bit in the thrall of Laura for a short time? Yep, you guessed it, although I wasn't nearly in the catatonic state of Snake Charmer.

Having Snake Charmer and Dirk in the foursome shielded Ingrid and Laura from enduring the kinds of *sorties* from male hikers that other female hikers habitually face. And foursome, not a fivesome, is what it would remain. I never was able to crack this group's *omerta code.*

That was okay, though. My hiking style had always been a bit nomadic—to bounce from one group to another, and often hike alone as well. Most importantly, though, was that my feet were finally feeling better. Given that 2,000 trail miles lay ahead, I was cautiously optimistic for the first time in a good while.

Chapter 17

Final Desert Surprises

Don't believe anything you hear, and only half of what you see.

Mark Twain

"Is THERE ANY WATER? EXCUSE ME. IS THERE ANY
WATER?" I yelled at the top of my lungs.

I was hiking alone at dusk. As was always the case as night
approached, I was wondering where I was going to camp and
get water. The Joshua Tree Spring was listed as having water and
campsites. Normally, this would have been a no-brainer. On this
occasion, however, there was a strange new issue.

Yogi's generally accurate guidebook had an odd note for
Joshua Tree Spring: "2005 hikers reported that a bear lives at this
spring."

A bear living in the desert? Wouldn't that be like seeing an
alligator in Alaska or a penguin in Kansas? Granted, our water
reports showed that the only water in the area was the swampy
water at the Joshua Tree Spring. Did I really want to go try to
spend the night where a bear might be living? I decided on
yelling down there with the ostensible purpose of finding out
about water. Finally, I heard a faint voice several hundred yards
down a hill yell back, "Yes." That settled it. This was my stopping
point for the day, and I headed down there.

Carlos and Gabe, both members of the University of Colorado track team that I had met yesterday, were sitting there eating dinner when I arrived. But they hadn't set up their tents yet.

"Skywalker," Carlos said. "We wondered if that was your voice."

"Yeah, how's the water?" I asked expectantly.

"Well, you can take a look," Carlos said wearily. "It's over in that heavy grass."

I dropped my food bag next to them, but then greed got the best out of me. I quietly walked over and found the flattest spot to pitch my tent.

"Hey, Skywalker," Carlos called out in a conversational manner, "Look, there's a bear."

He wasn't kidding. A large bear had slowly clambered up about 100 feet away, and begun drinking water out of a tub full of grotesque water. Besides the fact we were looking at a bear in the desert, the strangest thing was its color—cinnamon. Nonetheless, the people in the West routinely refer to their bears as black bears. It all made me wonder.

California once crawled with grizzlies—by some estimates 125,000. The natives maintained an uneasy truce with them. Western settlers countenanced no such accommodation, however, and fanatically hunted the grizzly. By the early twentieth century, the grizzly was completely extinct in California (although the grizzly remains on the state flag). But why was this bear more the color of a grizzly bear, as opposed to the jet-black bears found in the East? Did it have to do with the stronger sunlight in the West? Maybe. Or was it because the grizzlies had interbred with other bears, and hybrid strains of the grizzly remain in California?

Carlos and Gabe didn't seem worried and pulled their cameras out to snap some photographs. But then the bear started slowly sauntering in their direction, which black bears aren't supposed to do. They quickly started stuffing their food bags away into their backpacks.

"Will you grab my food bag?" I yelled to them.

"Yes, we got it."

The bear very slowly, but very surely, kept approaching them as they went into a quick retreat. Now they and the bear were headed in the direction of my tent.

My previous record for breaking down my tent was probably about three minutes. I demolished that record right here, as I frantically stuffed various parts into my backpack. But everything didn't fit in there when done in such grab-bag fashion.

"Hey, can you carry a couple of these parts," I quickly said to Carlos and Gabe, handing them tent poles and water. Petrified, we all tore up the hill.

Then the strangest thing happened. The bear had now gotten within twenty feet of us and we were completely on the lam. Suddenly and inexplicably, however, it turned on a dime and tore away like a scared rabbit. I had always heard bears are good climbers, but couldn't believe my eyes. This bear shot up a tree like a squirrel, without the slightest hesitation. At that point Carlos and Gabe began flinging rocks at it.

We raced up the hill in the dark and found our way to the intersection with the PCT. The next mile was the fastest I'd ever hiked, trying to keep up with these two athletes. I just kept my headlamp focused right on Gabe's heels and didn't say a word.

"Hey, what about here," I said pointing to an open spot just off the trail.

"Do you think this is far enough?' Carlos said.

"Yes," I answered. "That was a neighborhood bear. He hangs out in that swampy area."

"I'm cowboy camping," he immediately announced. "I want to be able to hear him if he shows up again."

***

Those who say you can fall in love at first sight are right, after all. I can tell you the minute I fell in love on the PCT.

It was the morning after the chilling bear encounter; Carlos and Gabe had hardly slept a wink.

"I'm not spending another night out here without my bear canister," Carlos had announced. The two of them blasted off to hike the remaining forty miles to Kennedy Meadows, where our bear canisters were waiting.

I was hiking alone and in a fragile frame of mind, myself. Obviously, I hadn't gotten the water I had hoped for last night at Joshua Tree Spring. Then, this morning I had passed the first branch of Spanish Needle Creek which was soggy, but not running. I wasn't desperately low on water, but I was worried. It was now the middle of June and boiling hot.

One of the things I found most eerie about the whole desert experience was that there were virtually no section hikers. The only people out here were PCT thru-hikers. It was almost like the only reason a person would be walking through here is because he or she had to be; anybody else would have to be crazy. However, I began to hear the murmur of human voices. It was a group of six very senior citizens heading southbound.

After swapping salutations, I quickly popped the question. "Is there any water up ahead?"

"Yes," answered a tall, thin male who appeared to be well into his seventies. "just before the left turn in about a half-mile, you will see a steady trickle up to your right. Get all you need there because there isn't any more for about twenty miles."

"Just what I needed to know," I said. "By the way, are you planning to get water at Joshua Tree Spring?"

"Yes, we're gonna' camp there tonight," he said.

"Well," I hesitated. "You might want to reconsider. A bear ran me and two other guys out of there last night at dark."

"Last night?" a minute-sized, elderly lady confirmed. "At Joshua Tree Spring."

"Yeah, my guidebook actually said the bear lived there, so if you camp there he's bound to turn up again." They looked around at each other with an odd sigh, here or there.

"Well, we'll figure out somewhere else to camp," the tall guy said stoically.

With that they all trudged wearily on.

The reason I immediately felt myself shot through with Cupid's arrow probably had to do with having lived in Florida the previous two years and, before that, working in a retirement home in Columbus, Georgia. From what I had seen, the primary trend for retirees is towards passivity and hostility to the unfamiliar. It's just human nature. This group could have been down in Florida or Arizona clipping coupons and complaining about the stock market. Instead, they had carved out a trail section that was plenty ambitious for them, and were going about it with their own brand of flair. Section hikers often get over-shadowed by flashier, more egocentric thru-hikers. But the more of them I see, the more impressed I've become of the equally worthy nature of their challenges.

***

Excitement was pulsing through the trail as we neared the critical mile 703 point. There, of course, the landscape would dramatically change. All kinds of rumors were flying around about the critical variant—the snowpack levels in the High Sierra. But then I ran into Chopper and Savior.

"We're out of food," Chopper said. *Out of food. We're still thirty miles from Kennedy Meadows. There is nothing between here and there.* What's more, he said it in a conversational manner.

Chopper and Savior were, of course, the two brothers who had run out of water the first day on the trail, at which point Chopper had been helicoptered out after hitting his SPOT button. *Murphy's Law* seemed to literally stalk them. All along the way I had been hearing about their mishaps and exploits. Now I had come upon them lying off to the side of the trail and spontaneously decided to take my lunch break right there. Bad decision.

I'm embarrassed to say I hesitated before deciding what to do. Of course, there is no real decision here. Besides, I was planning to make it to Kennedy Meadows in about 30 hours, and estimated I had two days worth of food. So I judiciously ladled out a few food items to each one. The way they said thanks reminded me of a politician seeking votes. They were good at this.

We all ate some lunch, and began hiking along together. They were really quite colorful, and seemingly very knowledgeable on all manner of outdoor topics. I walked along listening respectfully.

Then we came upon one of the most popular people on the

trail, *Attila*. He was a scrawny little fellow with a dark-black ayatollah beard, and a lightning quick hiker. Attila had just completed his doctorate in hydrology. I loved listening to him converse on a variety of water issues. What made him especially popular though, was the large bong packed away in his backpack. It was named after Attila the Hun, because of all the punishment it meted out.

Attila had been loading up his bong when Chopper, Savior, and I approached.

"Skywalker," Attila said, proffering the bong in a good-natured manner.

"Thank you," I laughed. "But hiking is difficult enough as it is."

Chopper and Savior weren't daunted one bit, however. Ten minutes later they lay with their heads on their backpacks, and minds back in the Stone Age. Next came a ravenous case of the munchies, as Chopper and Savior tore through every morsel of food I had just given them a couple hours ago. Reluctantly, I parceled out a few more spare items to them. Then, I quickly headed off alone, to protect my remaining food!

I was thinking about camping at Fox Mill Spring, tonight. However, the closer and closer we were getting to the mountains, the more moist areas were appearing. The swampy spring area here reminded me almost exactly of Joshua Tree Spring last night. Worried that I might again have the same hungry company as the previous evening if I camped here, I continued on.

Soon I was back in a more desert-looking area. At dark, I found a place to pitch my tent between some chapparal bushes for my last night in the desert. It was a typical spartan desert setting. However, in the middle of the night I heard a loud, spine-tingling screech, perhaps a hundred yards away. Then another shriek. *Cougar.*

I wasn't about to stick my head out of my tent. Instead, I lay inside paying rapt attention. However, I did hear footsteps of something running down the hill; in fact, it was running much faster than anything I'd ever heard. Blood-curdling screeches continued all the way down into the valley. Assuming it was a cougar, its screeches might have been to terrify the competition and establish territory. Or perhaps it was just thirsty and running down the hill for a midnight drink of water.

Like most hikers, I had both loved and hated the desert passionately. One thing was for sure, though. I was never going to forget it.

Chapter 18

Going Up

"Good gosh," I said frustrated, "what good does this thing do if it protects your food from a bear, but I can't get in the damn thing myself."

"You can usually open it this way," Snake Charmer patiently said. He took out a knife and pressed down on the tab. Slowly, he unscrewed the top of my bear canister. Now I had to figure out just how much food I could stuff in there. Then came the worst part— jamming the awful thing in my backpack.

"Skywalker," Ingrid said. "Try some of these German chocolates."

"Thanks."

"Here Skywalker," Laura rushed over to say. "Take these Lara bars. They cost too much to throw them away."

"Well, if I've got room."

Kennedy Meadows is a small, lonely redoubt at the foot of the *High Sierra*. Like everybody else, I had sent a food drop here because of the lack of available supplies. But if I had to do it over again, I don't think I would send anything. Hikers had wildly over-shipped food here. People I had never seen before were trying to hand off dehydrated meals. The sad thing is that several days from now in the most remote mountainous areas, when everybody was running low on food, they would have paid a pretty penny to get this food back. But here at Kennedy Meadows they couldn't fit it all into their bear canisters.

"Bears are a bigger part of hiking in the West than the East," everybody kept saying. "They're smarter and more aggressive." Hiking trails are full of bear experts. From what I'd seen, though, you simply couldn't make sweeping projections about bears. Most of them seemed to have quite different temperaments and personalities. The one three nights ago had surprised us twice; first, with its boldness, and then its inexplicable flight in fear.

These self-anointed bear experts did have one undeniably valid point, though. Because of the extreme aridity in the West, vegetation is not as dense. Since bears are 80% vegetarian, they have much less to eat. They make up for it by becoming more aggressive in trying to steal hiker food. It's not irrational. All the plants and logs and berries bears gnaw on all day have low-calories densities. But, if they can get their paws on a hiker food bag, they can score 15,000 or 20,000 calories in a jiffy. So stealing hiker food is only rational. But given that you were often days away from an emergency bailout, it was a disquieting prospect.

***

Nevada is a spanish word meaning snowy. By that translation, the state of Nevada's name is an abomination. It is the second driest state in the United States (only Arizona is drier). On the other hand, the early Spanish explorers named this mountain range ahead, *The Sierra Nevada*. It means "snowy mountain range." They got that dead right.

The annual snowfall in the Sierras is several times that of the Rockies. Some of it—a lot of it actually—never even melts. Other parts don't melt until late July or August. This can be problematic to the point of dangerous for PCT hikers.

A couple weeks earlier, while it was raining on us in the Mojave Desert, a heavy snowstorm had hit the Sierras. The early pack of hikers into the Sierras had been forced to retrace their steps back to the safe haven of the Kennedy Meadows Campground. A lower-than-average snow year had now turned into an average snow year. Fair enough. When in the Sierras, hike in the snow.

The landscape immediately changed. In place of scraggly desert bushes covering a relentlessly brown and stucco landscape, we were now engulfed by lush green meadows and bursting flowers. It was a welcome change. My mood was an excitement, filled with trepidation. In fact, this day—entering the High Sierra—was a day I had been anticipating for years.

The ascent was slow at first. White-capped peaks appeared in the distance. Of course, it was the snowmelt from those same peaks that had created this brilliantly verdant setting.

My new hiking partner, CanaDoug, a stocky, 53 year-old Canadian, and I arrived in Menarche Meadows. It was a beautiful, wide-open meadow, but nakedly exposed to a strong current. Immediately, I made a bone-headed mistake.

The Kern River flowed out of the mountains and through Menarche Meadows, in an almost lyrically beautiful way.

"Hey, that sand bar along the river looks perfect for our tents," I said to CanaDoug.

"Are you kidding?" CanaDoug asked.

"But shouldn't the wind die down at dark?" I asked hopefully.

"I don't know," he said skeptically. "I'm going up on that hill."

I pitched my tent on the sand bar, only to be clobbered by gales of wind all night. No sleep. Bad start.

I followed that up by getting lost second thing next morning. Head down and leaning forward into the powerful current, I had barged across Menarche Meadows and was happy to get to tree cover. But then I went the wrong way.

Every other time I had been lost, I would simply backtrack angrily and soon find out where I had blundered. But here I thrashed determinedly straight up the bank of a creek, surprised at how rugged and steep the trail had become. A grave feeling set in. This wasn't a careless mistake. When you worry constantly about something for days and weeks, even months and years, but it happens anyway, it takes on a different type of gravity. Not anger, because you were doing your damndest to avoid it. A more profound negative feeling sets in. *Maybe I'm in over my head.*

I kept walking. Finally, I came upon a well-maintained trail running at a right angle to the direction I was climbing. But I had no idea if it was the PCT. Unlike the desert, the Sierras have an extensive network of hiking trails. And if this was the PCT, should I go left or right? I went left and soon came to a fork.

I dropped my backpack and spent almost an hour running sorties in various directions. But I worried about straying too far from my backpack, given the bear-dense environment. My reconnaisance only left me more confused. Finally, I decided to sit down and eat lunch, and hope another hiker came along.

I soon heard singing. That meant it was probably Backtrack, the brainy college professor from Alaska. What a study in contradictions this man was. He had an utter fear of bears.

"If I saw a bear," he insisted, "I would feel like I've done something wrong."

"I thought Alaskans treated 'em like pets," I said surprised.

"No," he corrected me, "I had a friend in Alaska that got attacked and killed by a bear while riding his bicycle."

Despite this, Backtrack hiked at night more than anyone else. He compensated by keeping up a lively repertoire of evening tunes.

"Where in the world is the PCT?" I asked Backtrack. "You're sitting on it," he said.

"That way," I started down the hill to the left.

"No, this way," he headed right up the hill. The only solace I could find from my haplessness was that *Backtrack* had gotten his own trail name from similar mishaps.

We soon came upon CanaDoug, who had corralled three other hikers who had taken the same errant route as me.

"Skywalker," CanaDoug laughed, "you're lucky you took the wrong trail. I ran into a big bear—350 pounder—right on the PCT."

"Oh great, he must have wandered down from Canada."

"We've already decided," CanaDoug said in pep-talk fashion, "everybody needs to hang with another person, at least until we get through these mountains."

That was music to my ears. As I was to see on several occasions further along, this rugged Canadian had some latent leadership skills that surfaced on impromptu occasions.

Chapter 19

Two-Miles High

Being over 10,000 feet takes some getting used to. There is the obvious reason—the air is thinner. I seemed to do alright here, while others gasped, as we climbed and climbed the second and third day into the Sierras. Maybe the years I had spent getting and staying in shape for this trail were helping.

The cold was another story. It must be noted that mammals living in cold climates (ex. polar bears) tend to be short-limbed and thick trunked. Humans can adapt over time, as well. Eskimos are the most short-limbed people on this planet. This minimizes the surface area and helps them retain heat. Giraffes, on the other hand, have massive surface areas, which makes it difficult to retain heat. Surely not coincidentally, this is why they are found exclusively in warmer climes. Thousands of lame giraffe jokes over the years aside, it is obviously the animal I most closely resemble.

The weather is almost always perfect this time of year in the Sierras. But when the sun goes down, the temperature plummets forty or more degrees. I was to spend a total of ten nights camped above ten thousand feet, and the pattern was always the same—start the night off reasonably warm and end up shivering in seven layers of clothing.

On the third day, we entered Sequoia National Park, where the scenery bordered on ethereal. Being from Georgia, I was partial to pine trees to begin with. But I had never seen anything like these gigantic Sequoia trees. In fact, they are the largest living things on this planet (a few things in the ocean are bigger). Sequoias can measure over 300 feet in height and have been around since Biblical times. California's redwood trees, found in the coastal region, are actually taller, but Sequoias have much larger trunks and branches. Despite their weight being in the neighborhood of two-and-a-half million pounds, they retain a graceful beauty about them. It doesn't take a dewy-eyed tree hugger to realize that cutting them down would be worse than a crime.

That evening we arrived at Chicken Spring Lake, a gorgeous alpine lake that had obviously been fed from the snowmelt in the mountains hovering steeply on three sides of it. I just took my nalgene bottle and dipped it straight into the lake for a drink. Attila was on hand and rhapsodic at the whole scene.

"I didn't expect to see you again," I said to the fleet-footed hydrologist.

"Oh man," he said wondrously, "a place like this shows the world has hope."

Attila had gotten here last night and spent all day just gazing at the water. He would repeat this habit of taking a zero day at the best water sources all the way to Canada.

"But bundle up," he added, "it got down to seventeen last night."

Although I obsessed over the approaching cold night, the excitement was palpable around the campsite as a dozen-and-a-half of our comrades arrived on the scene. Mount Whitney, the highest point in the contiguous United States, was only two days away.

Luna, the young girl I had seen at various points along the way, was also on hand.

"Skywalker," she asked, "are you going up Mount Whitney (Mount Whitney is actually a side trail off the PCT)?"

"No," I said. "I don't have an ice axe."

"Oh, come on now," she scoffed. "You're going up with me."

I would have loved to have climbed a marquee mountain such as Mount Whitney, but it would add an extra day-and-a-half before getting to the next food re-supply point. But I was soon to find out that, for whatever reason, this young girl wanted me to summit Whitney even more than I did.

***

"It's a little sketchy in a few places," Dirk said.

There was that damn word *sketchy* again. Hikers loved to use it. But I would soon learn to fear this god-awful word, whenever I heard it. For whatever reason—perhaps not to appear cowardly— hikers don't like to say the word "dangerous. So they use "sketchy."

Dirk, Snake Charmer, and Laura, were descending from Mount Whitney as we were headed up to the ranger's base camp. Ingrid had sensibly chosen not to go up because she was having breathing problems at this altitude. The other three looked flushed in the face. We've all seen that kind of flushed look before.

"Why don't we start up at three in the morning," CanaDoug suddenly suggested to everyone at base camp.

"Why?" I asked perplexed.

"We could watch the sunrise from the summit."

"Man, that would be cool," said Donovan and several other hikers.

"Come on, Skywalker," Doug exhorted me.

"Forget it," I said, uncharacteristically decisive. "I may try for the summit tomorrow morning."

"You're going up," Luna again insisted. "I'm not taking no for an answer."

"I don't know if I have enough food for the extra day," I grumbled.

"You will be fed, Skywalker," HWAP said amused.

All I knew is I'd be shivering all night here at the base camp, which was at 11,500 feet, and higher than I'd ever been in my 48 years. By contrast, Clingman's Dome, the highest point on the entire Appalachian Trail, measures 6,700 feet.

I expected to hear all kinds of racket in the middle of night as everyone headed off. But to my surprise, I heard nothing. And it sure wasn't because I was sound asleep. When I emerged from my tent, there was CanaDoug.

"My foot's really banged up," said Canadoug. "I'm giving it a rest today."

Sitting next to him was Spare Parts, an older guy who had practically killed himself the last few weeks straining to keep up with Luna. Because Mount Whitney is not part of the official PCT, he was also planning to rest in his tent all day.

"That leaves you and me, Skywalker," Luna said confidently. "Are you about ready?"

***

Luna was a physical specimen, pure and simple. I honestly don't say that in a prurient sense. Describing her any other way would be like trying to describe me without using the word tall. She was of Scandinavian ancestry and had the type physique one routinely sees in winter Olympic athletes. She also had the most upright, purest stride I've ever seen in a hiker. I was sentenced to trying to keep up with her the entire day. And that—putting in your maximum effort, or more commonly said, 'hiking your ass off'—isn't necessarily a good idea at such high elevations.

I halfway expected Luna to zoom ahead out of view, at which point I could decide whether to continue, or turn around. But every time it looked like it might happen, she would stop and wait on me.

We ascended a thousand feet to Guitar Lake, which is referred to by mountaineers as a *tarn*. Many of these alpine lakes remain a turquoise-colored ice, year-round. However, Guitar Lake gets enough sun for it to melt into crystal clear water. I dipped my nalgene bottle in and drank what was undoubtedly some of the best water in the world. Dark-brown marmots, that could easily be mistaken for raccoons or rabbits, were doing somersaults all over the boulders surrounding the lake. In fact, the next couple weeks I was to notice that the higher the elevation, the more marmots we saw. They are obviously especially well-insulated animals.

"Are all these marmot jackets and sleeping bags we use made of actual marmots?" I asked several people. I was hoping the answer was yes, but nobody really seemed to know.

Several hikers had camped right here at Guitar Lake last

night. This would have been hugely advantageous to camp this far up, and I had considered it. But I had worried the extreme cold would overwhelm my lean frame.

Luna and I started up. The trail ran sideways along ridges and was covered with snow and ice. I assumed as low of a crouch (not exactly my forte) as possible, and tentatively began traversing zigzags up the mountain.

"Luna," I gasped. "I'm holding you up. Go on ahead."

"Shut up and keep hiking," she barked.

I kept hiking, but remained schizophrenic about the entire endeavor. *This isn't part of the PCT. I don't have to do this.*

My head felt like the sun was boring a hole right through my skull. I had just finished reading Jon Krakauer's book, *Into Thin Air*. In it, he had vividly described the headaches that oxygen-deprived mountaineers get at higher elevations. Krakauer had mentioned that mountaineers frequently attempted to relieve headaches by putting snow on top of their heads. I loaded up my baseball cap with snow and placed it on my head, which brought some temporary relief.

I had only brought one water bottle from base camp, and was rapidly drinking it down in the glaring, early-afternoon sun. My rationale had been that there was snow everywhere, so why lug a bunch of water up to the top. However, I had also heard, "Watch out for the *pink snow*." Veteran mountaineers have reams of tales of violently being laid low by contaminated, pink algae snow. Nonetheless, I began stuffing my nalgene bottle full of snow and gulping the contents down.

A man and his teenage daughter came from the opposing direction.

"Excuse me sir," I anxiously asked. "About how far is it to the top?"

He seemed to pick up the concern in my voice and chose to answer in an empathetic way.

"You've done the worst," he said. "Well," he corrected himself, "actually you have a couple more icy ridges ahead, but then it levels out close to the top."

"How long 'til we get to where it evens out?"

The High Sierras rock. Better yet, the PCT hiker covers the very most wondrous parts.

"Oh, you should be up there in about fifteen minutes," he assured me.

Some people low-ball you in situations like that, and others (like me) are more likely to high-ball you. Perhaps Freud could figure out why. All I know is that this guy had dramatically understated the amount of time ahead.

Soon, I was exhausted again.

"Luna, honestly," I pleaded, "If you fall here, you've bought it. I'm not a professional climber. It doesn't make sense to take so much risk."

"You're going to the top with me, Skywalker," she said unflinchingly. "In fact, you're leading me up there because I'm hiking behind you the rest of the way up."

Luna was an unlikely *trail Nazi*. But that's what this was turning into—a forced march.

"I've got to take a break," I said firmly and lay down on the snow.

I slowly began picking at some food and gulping down Advil. Soon some our comrades arrived in high spirits as they were descending down Whitney. Normally quite voluble in all these shoestring conversations on the trail, I lay there comatose as Luna entertained.

"What did you do to him?" Five Dollar asked.

"Oh, he's just playing possum," Luna said merrily.

"Watch out for that right turn up ahead," Five Dollar said in the first serious comment I'd ever heard him make. "It's really icy."

"We've got to get going, Skywalker," Luna said. "Do you want to get caught in the dark on Whitney?"

"I'm going back down with them," I said, without really meaning it.

"No, you're not," she cut me off. "Get your you-know-what moving."

It was now a matter of just executing the best I could. There were two steep ridges that were completely flat, but iced over. If you slipped, you were *home-free*. I quickly took to my knees and groveled across the iciest parts. Obviously, I wasn't going to win the Edmund Hilary Stiff-Upper-Lip-Award, but at least I was through complaining. Luna could only carry me so far.

Eventually, we arrived at the flat area, although every time I saw something resembling an icy ridge, tremors pulsed through me. We bore into the stiff, cutting wind, and there were a couple more snowfields as we neared the top. Finally, we arrived at the summit of Mount Whitney about 3:00. It had taken us five hours.

***

Mount Whitney, at 14,494 feet, is the most awesome landscape I've ever had the privilege to behold. It reminded me of the moving footage of Brad Pitt and company in the film, *Seven Years in Tibet*— white capped mountain range after range, *ad infinitum* into the distance. Actually, there had been considerable speculation in the past that Mount Whitney was actually not the tallest mountain in the Lower Forty-Eight. Somewhere in this sea of soaring peaks I was looking at was a lonely mountain a few feet taller. But—so the story goes—the National Park Service and U.S. Forest Service don't want to publicize it because a whole tourism industry is built around Mount Whitney.

Luna sat there celebrating and snapping photos with John Muir Trail Hikers (The fabulous—and highly recommended by this hiker— John Muir Trail ends at Whitney summit). Meanwhile, I just lay there with an awful headache, worried about the coming descent. The only thing that motivated me was I had to take an emergency crap. As we had left Crabtree Meadow this morning for Mount Whitney, Luna and I had passed a receptacle with small sacks. You were supposed to use these to pack out any bowel movements you might have on Whitney. It was obviously desirable that pristine Mount Whitney not look like human-sized geese had invaded it. But Luna and I had hurried right past it.

I walked sullenly over behind the emergency hut on the Whitney summit. Here, I quickly laid a *deuce* in the snow. Obviously, that won't win me any trail good citizenship award, but—believe me—I didn't have any jurisdiction in the matter at this point.

"Let's go, Luna," I kept urging her. "It's almost four."

But she was a fish in water to my fish out of water on Whitney summit, and kept on socializing. Finally, everybody left except us.

We were quite lucky, to be honest. Violent electrical storms are very common on Mount Whitney late on summer afternoons and have aborted many a climb to Whitney's summit; several people have even been struck and died over the years. The weather could have changed on a dime. But it didn't.

Luna and I started down. I didn't think we would pass anybody still climbing this late in the afternoon. But in the distance appeared a lone female figure trudging to the top. When she got up to us, it appeared this lady was pushing sixty.

"Excuse me," this woman asked us, "how much longer do I have to reach the summit?"

"Forty-five minutes max," I quickly said.

"Forty-five minutes," she gasped, "It's just right there."

"Less," Luna said sympathetically.

"Forty-five minutes max," I said. I honestly thought it was best to not lead her on with a low-ball. She looked worried, but soldiered on.

We soon came up on the John Muir Trail hikers, who were all gathered around a gigantic crevasse in the snow. Worse yet, it was right where we would ordinarily walk.

"What the hell happened here?" I asked.

"It looks like a horse, or something, might have fallen through," one of them laughed.

"Man, if you fell in there," I exclaimed, "how would you ever get out?"

All I know is I became especially careful, gingerly planting my steps on solid snow to avoid this most dreadful of possibilities. It was late June after all.

The icy patches and steep falloffs were every bit as daunting while descending. But now I had a psychological tailwind, and we made good time back to Guitar Lake.

"I'm washing my hair," Luna immediately said, and headed straight over to the crystal clear tarn to submerge her head.

"You're next," she announced when she pulled her head out. I put up a tepid argument, but quickly caved. Magically, the bitter cold water devastated my headache, and I was able to hike at maximum speed with Luna back down to base camp.

Luna had obviously found the perfect combination of humiliation and encouragement (heavily weighted towards the former!) to get me to Whitney summit. I'll leave it up to the reader to decide whether or not I would have made it to the top without her.

Chapter 20

"Fifty Feet"

If at first you don't succeed, parachuting is probably not for you.

Old saying

Stupidity can run amok in groups, especially after having been out for so many days and with everybody running low on food.

It was two days later and we were facing Forrester's Pass, the highest point on the actual PCT at 13,180 feet. The minute a person begins planning a PCT hike, you hear about Forrester's Pass. Yesterday afternoon, CanaDoug and I had forded ice-cold Tindall Creek and camped with others along its banks. Some hikers had seemed tight as a tick. However, summiting Mount Whitney seemed to have temporarily inoculated me. I was uncharacteristically serene about what lay ahead.

CanaDoug had eagerly bolted out of camp this morning. He seemed especially determined after having missed Mount Whitney. Usually, I could catch up with him. But this morning he was in a fly pattern. So was everybody else for that matter. It made no sense. Speaker after speaker at the Kickoff had reiterated what Yogi had emphasized in her guidebook:

"Try to plan your days in the Sierra so you are *not* crossing a pass early in the morning. You must give the snow time to soften. If you're there too early in the day, you will be walking on ice."

Indeed, it seemed especially important to heed that advice on this occasion. Back at the Whitney base camp, a ranger had told a group of us, "There's about fifty feet of *black ice* right at the top of Forrester Pass. That's where it gets sketchy."

Sketchy.

I rushed for miles through snow and rock fields trying to catch up with everyone. A giant wall of granite running at virtually a right angle appeared ahead a few miles in front of us. Somewhere in there was an opening—albeit narrow and icy— that was the pass we needed to get through this large monolith. It was difficult to tell exactly where because the sun wasn't peering over the granite wall yet. But nobody was a waitin'.

A couple days before, a woman named Pepperoni, who was attempting to become the first woman to ever ride a horse the entire PCT, had arrived at the foot of Forrester's Pass. She actually had two horses tied together (one for carrying supplies). But when she had craned her neck up at this steep, snowy ascent, she didn't like what she saw. Neither did her horses which became balky and unruly. Pepperoni decided it would be virtually suicidal for her horses to attempt to clear Forrester's Pass. Unfortunately, she had to retrace every single foot she and her horses had covered the last two days, to bail out all the way back at Cottonwood Pass. It may have been the best decision she ever made.

"This way," Big John said when I finally caught up with everyone. He then started straight up a snowbank. The big lumberjack boots Big John wore—which would eventually lead to his downfall on the PCT—worked wonders here in the deep snow. He started straight up a steep, icy snow field. CanaDoug went next, followed by me.

I can't believe this. The PCT isn't supposed to have climbs this steep. In fact, it doesn't. But it wasn't until a couple months later in Oregon when we were recounting the whole episode, that I found out this escarpment we were scaling wasn't the PCT after all. Big John was as down-to-earth of a guy as you could find; but maybe he couldn't resist showboating what he could do in his big boots.

"Hold on, Skywalker," CanaDoug yelled back as I rushed right up on him. "If I go down, I'm gonna bring you with me."

"Yeah, yeah," I would nervously say, and drop back.

But then anxiety and adrenalin would catapult me forward, and I'd be right on his tail again. A fall would have been disastrous for both of us.

Finally, we got to a switchback and I was relieved to resume its meandering route up to the top of the pass. Our climb straight up the face of the mountain had been a fool's errand. But it wasn't as dangerous as what lay right up ahead.

***

A few days earlier a Canadian hiker named Andrew Dawson had arrived at the sheet of black ice at Forrester's Pass. Not only did Andrew have an utter phobia of the U.S. government, but he was an unapologetic socialist. He simply did not believe in capitalism. Or at least, he didn't think he believed in capitalism until he arrived at Forrester's Pass.

Andrew had an ice axe attached to his backpack and was a skilled outdoorsman. He used it to easily traverse the sheet of black ice. While he had been in the act of crossing, a middle-aged southbound hiker had walked up to the sheet of ice from the opposite direction; he was petrified by what he saw.

"Excuse me sir," he anxiously said to Andrew, who was half his age. "Now that you've crossed over, are you going to need that ice axe."

"I might need it for a few more of the passes," Andrew had replied.

"Is there any way I could buy it from you?" the man had suggested, "You can buy one when you get to the next trail town?"

Andrew had about ten dollars to his name at this point, and

it had been that way for a couple hundred miles. He was a master at living off the food found in hiker boxes in trail towns.

"Yeah," Andrew had answered cagily. "We might be able to do something like that."

"Here," the man had said fumbling through a wad of bills. "Here's $100 (more than a new ice axe costs)."

"Uh," Andrew paused, "I think $200 is probably about right."

The exchange was made and they headed separate ways. The world has marveled the last few decades at how adeptly Chinese communists have learned capitalism. But Canadian socialists are quick learners, too!

***

"I don't think you'd die if you fell here," said another Canadian, Josephine, when she arrived at the ice sheet.

"That's exactly what I was just thinking," I responded. Which tells you a little bit about what I was really thinking!

Josephine was now right in front of me, and also the only person who was wearing crampons attached to her shoes. Everybody had bunched up in a single-file line. I quickly saw why. It was the fifty *feet* from hell—black ice with a steep, bald dropoff for hundreds of feet. And it was all the blacker looking because the sun still hadn't cleared the granite monolith that towered above us.

Attila was the first to go over and made it without much sweat. One by one hikers slowly made their way across as I watched intently. I was worried that I had only one ski pole to everybody else's two trekking poles. But my biggest concern, far and away, was my high center of gravity. It's no accident that great gymnasts are on the lower end of the Bell Curve of height.

"Easy does it, Skywalker," Attila called over, when my turn to cross came.

I crouched down as low as I could, choked up the grip of ski pole and continually stabbed the ground as I walked very slowly. After about twenty feet I realized the problems wasn't as much fifty feet of black ice; it was *five feet*.

I couldn't figure out anywhere to put my foot on my next

step to gain traction. It all looked like either shaved snow or ice. I stood there frozen. *If I had young kids, I simply wouldn't do this. I'd turn around like Pepperoni had and walk backwards for two days.* No lyin'.

Normally, you try to step upwards to gain some purchase, but the only spot that looked like it might have some pliable snow was about a foot downhill. But I might not be able to brake after that step. "There's nowhere to go uphill," I yelled to Attila. "Should I take a step downhill?"

"No," he quickly yelled.

That settled it. I wasn't going to turn around, and I wasn't going to take a step downhill.

"Sometimes you just have to trust the traction in your shoes," I had heard someone say a couple days ago.

I would trust my shoes. I bent into the mountain and grabbed at the ice on the bank above with my right hand. Soon I was across the sheet of black ice, although I honestly am not completely confident the result would be the same if I ever attempted it again.

Hikers generally don't like to show jubilation and they didn't here. But there was a palpable relief in the air as we stood on the top of Forrester's Pass taking photographs, even though deep snow fields lay ahead.

The other side of Forrester Pass was packed with snow, but not harrowing, and everyone laboriously postholed through the field. To my amazement CanaDoug, Miles, and Hat Man spotted a gorgeous alpine lake down a hill to the left and decided to jump in naked. Attila, meanwhile, was torn. If there was one hiker on the trail thinner and less insulated than me, it was him.

"Man, I don't know if I should do this," he said as the other three were running down to strip off their clothes.

"God, it would be suicidal for me," I said.

"Aw, what the hell," he said undeterred, and began making his way down the hill.

The first three were well built, but hopped out like ants the minute they hit the water. But when Attila landed, it was like he had jumped on a burning stove he was up and out of there so fast.

Their Sierra adventures continued when they got their clothes back on. We rounded a turn in the trail and were confronted with an especially steep descent down a snowy slope. However, there was a narrow path going straight down the hill where hikers had obviously *glissaded* (slide on your butt).

"I love to glissade!" Yogi had declared in her handbook. "It's also not very smart."

Nonetheless, CanaDoug went barreling down

CanaDoug glissades furiously down Forrester's Pass, while I stand there more confused than ever.

as he emitted some incomprehensible Canadian scream of ecstasy. Everybody immediately followed. Then it was my turn again. Unlike the black ice back at Forrester Pass, glissading was not something I absolutely had to do. So I began trying to sidestep down the bank of snow which ended up being not only exhausting, but fraught with its own perils. I was to quickly find out the Sierras had so many snow fields, it was necessary that I learn a controlled glissade.

Finally, we made it down to a flat enough area to take a long break. It was the seventh day out from Kennedy Meadows and the remaining pickings in my bear canister were slim indeed. Donovan had known I was running especially low on food.

"Hey Skywalker," he had asked yesterday, "Do you want this Ramen side?"

I had meekly accepted it, and savored every bite of the cold, hard noodles. Now I was within a day of resupply, and relieved about having successfully cleared Mount Whitney and Forrester Pass. Buying Donovan something in recompense when we got to a trail town simply wouldn't be the same as out here.

"How about this Power Bar?" I asked Dononvan.

"Well, if you're sure you don't need it," he said. I wanted it, but didn't absolutely need it. So I tossed it to him.

That night CanaDoug, Donovan, Josephine, and I camped in some open field after having descended 3,000 feet from Forrester's Pass. Our spirited conversation got cut short, however, as freezing rain, then snow, drove us into our tents.

What we had to do next was actually quite disheartening, in the scheme of things. To get to the trail town of Independence to resupply—which was absolutely essential—we had to take a side trail nine miles down a 2,500 foot descent. Of course, we would have to do the same thing in reverse after re-supplying, which meant 18 miles of walking and 5,000 feet of descents and ascents without making one inch of forward progress on the actual PCT.

Despite this, morale was high all around as town and hot food lay immediately ahead.

Chapter 21

Scott Williamson PCT Superstar

"You just missed Scott Williamson," No Pain said.

"Dammit," I anguished. "How fast was he going?"

"Not that much faster than everybody else," he said, surprised.

"Would he talk to anybody?"

"A little bit," No Pain said. "But he cut out pretty quickly."

Later in the day I came upon Backtrack.

"Guess who was at our campsite last night," he said.

"Who?"

"Scott Williamson."

"What time did he get there?" I asked.

"Right at dark."

"Did he take time to eat?" I wondered.

"A little bit," Backtrack said. "I gave him a Fig Newton."

"What was he like?"

"He came off as pretty normal," Backtrack said. "He talked about these green onions he pulls off trees."

"Did he have a tent?" I asked.

"No, he just threw his sleeping bag down right by the trail. He was gone by 5:00 this morning."

"Makes sense," I said.

Any intense endeavor is bounds to have its legends. The PCT is no exception. Scott Williamson is probably too young to be considered a legend. But he is hands-down the star of the trail.

***

On January 20th, 1996, 24 year-old Scott Williamson wasn't even supposed to be on duty. But the liquor store where he worked was short-handed, and he agreed to fill in. Late in the afternoon, a strange-looking man in a hooded sweatshirt entered the store and approached the counter. He kept rocking back and forth, and looked nervous. Scott soon found out why.

The man pulled a gun out and fired a bullet straight into the left side of Scott's face. Scott turned and ran to the back of the store, but the door was locked. He managed to bang it open with his shoulder and flee, while his assailant pursued and fired six more rounds at him. Some people in a nearby parking lot helped him get to the hospital where he was given morphine, and told his salivary gland might never function again. He had missed being paralyzed by ¼ inch. Unsurprisingly, this turned out to be the turning point in his life.

The PCT held out an especial allure for Scott. It had only a tiny fraction of the number of thru-hikers that the AT had at that point. Scott proceeded to thru-hike the PCT year after year—twelve times in total. But that wasn't all. When he got to the Canadian border, he habitually turned around and tried to walk all the way back to Mexico in the same year. For most hikers, including this one, the idea of arriving in Canada and then trying to reverse one's steps for the last 2,663 miles would be not only impossible, but utterly repugnant. In fact, nobody had ever completed such a *yo-yo* before.

The PCT's specific geography (late-melting summer snow in the Sierras, followed by new snow in the early fall) makes a yo-yo enormously complicated, even for a hiker of Scott's caliber. On multiple occasions, Scott was racing back south from Canada only to get caught in the snow in late October in the High Sierra. Each time he had to bail out to save his life. But this was to become an *Ahab-like* pursuit, and he only intensified his determination.

In October, 2004, it seemed like he was just a little bit ahead of schedule as he approached the critical Forrester's Pass. But snow clouds—and another disappointment—loomed on the horizon. This time, however, old Lady Luck smiled on him. Two hours after he cleared Forrester's Pass, the heavens opened up. Two climbers were killed in that snowstorm and several hiking groups were stranded and had to be rescued. Scott had to endure three straight days of heavy snowfall, but had cleared all the major mountain passes. On Nov. 18, 2004, he arrived at the Mexican border to complete his 5,320 mile journey.

Now, in 2009 he was attempting to break David Horton's PCT speed record of 66 days from Mexico to Canada. At the Kickoff, they had shown us a video of Scott hiking in the High Sierra.

"I keep bleeding out of my ears at the end of the day," he reported. In other words, he punishes himself out there into a zone that other thru-hikers are unfamiliar with. But he has another key asset, as well; he is one of the greatest *minimalists* ever.

The base weight of his backpack (everything but food and water) is only 8½ pounds. He has cut straps and everything remotely superfluous out of it, and doesn't carry a stove or a bear cannister through the High Sierra. The one area that he doesn't skimp on is food. "Some people are able to do the PCT on Ramen and Snickers bars," he said. "But I avoid sugar on the trail because sugar highs and crashes affect my hiking rhythms." Typically, a couple hours before he quits hiking, he puts some dehydrated refried beans in water, and mixes in some tortilla chips. Better yet, he augments his diet on the trail by foraging for wild onions and berries.

When Scott comes racing into trail towns to resupply, he's given the rock-star treatment. In fact, he's been forced to master the politician's art of showing interest in everybody that wants to talk to him, but effecting quick breakaways.

"When I first started doing it, it was just something I enjoyed," Scott recalls. "But as time goes by, I've found it gives people inspiration." That's about as bold of a comment as you're going to get from someone who is universally described as down- to-earth and humble.

Unfortunately, hiking is a lifestyle, but not a livelihood. In order to pursue his passion, Scott works hard in the off-season as a logger and construction worker.

"I don't own a home, I drive derelict vehicles. I have to work on every weekend. But the sacrifices I've made to get on that trail have been well worth it."

Needless to say, after missing Scott at Kearsage Pass, I never caught a glimpse of him. He went on to break the PCT speed record by hiking the entire 2,663 miles in 65 days and 8 hours. Better yet, he did it *unsupported* by any van—unlike previous record holders—and even refused rides into town to resupply. And he wasn't a hog about basking in the glory, either. Another fleet-footed, ferociously determined hiker named Adam Bradley asked to accompany Scott on the record-setting journey, and they stayed together the whole way. Better yet, upon completion who was amongst the first people the two new record holders called? None other than David Horton, the previous record holder. No, it wasn't a taunting message of one-upsmanship, but more like artists discussing their work.

A rebuttal would be welcome from anyone with alternative information. But my research didn't yield anything to contradict the conclusion that Scott Williamson is the greatest long-distance hiker of all time.

Chapter 22

CanaDoug—Snow Maven

You've got to know your body. Pure and simple.

CanaDoug and I stood at the foot of Glen Pass after having climbed 2,500 feet back up to the PCT at Kearsage Pass.

"I think I'll just camp right here," CanaDoug said to my surprise.

"But we were going over Glen Pass today," I said.

"It's too late," he said. "It'll take hours to get over."

Standing there setting up their tent was a twosome I hadn't seen before—*Lauren and Pat*. I really wanted to hike on. But here were three hikers of my ilk who thought it was too late to clear Glen Pass. I decided to respect their judgment.

The problem was that Pat and Lauren—and now CanaDoug—were camped on a rocky bluff with little room for my unfortunate-sized two-person tent. We were up here, too. I knew exactly how my body would react—use up lots of energy trying to stay warm, but with limited success.

"I'm going back a mile or two," I announced.

"Yeah, right," CanaDoug said.

"No," I maintained, "it'll be warmer. There was a perfect spot to camp back there." I picked up my stuff and, to everybody's amazement, started back down and south.

I got back down to where I had been just an hour ago, set up my tent, and placed my bear canister the obligatory fifty yards away from my tent. The canister was your worst enemy by day, but your best friend at night. Neither bears nor mice could get in there in any conceivable way. That was especially fortunate for this area, which was notoriously bear dense.

The rangers at a nearby ranger's station had recently attempted to supply the station with provisions for a few weeks. The experiment ended up stillborn, however. The first night after the station was supplied, a bear had ripped the metal roof right off the station before going in and demolishing every single bit of the food. Kinda' brings up the old saying—if you don't succeed at first, *don't* try again.

I urinated a ring around my tent, which reputedly helps repel bears. Then, I got in for what ended up being a rare good night's sleep in my tent, proving I did know a little something about my fickle body. At first light, I headed off and retraced the terrain I had given back late yesterday. Surprisingly, CanaDoug had already torn out of there, along with Pat.

Lauren and I slashed through the snowy switchbacks and banks to get up to the top of Glen Pass.

"Hey, this isn't so bad," I said, relieved when we cleared the summit.

"Yeah," Lauren said. "It's not that steep."

It was a wide snowfield to be sure, and there were two sets of hiker footprints, running at various angles. We followed the lower set of prints, which required staying in a crouch for a few hundred yards. But it proved to be more demanding, than harrowing. Finally, we came to a steep chute where CanaDoug and everybody had obviously glissaded. After roiling my quads for the last hour, the logic of glissading became overwhelming.

"Have you done this, yet?" I asked Lauren.

"Yeah, just stay on your butt and make sure your head doesn't flip around while you're sliding."

"Ladies first." Lauren slid down the steep chute, and I followed without great form—but without incident, and we were at the bottom of Glen Pass.

All these snowy passes had multiple lakes and snow at the bottom formed from the runoff, and Glen Pass was no exception. You knew you were going to be off the trail for sizable distances. The challenge was to not get too lost and stay in the vicinity of the trail. Once the snow gave way at lower elevations you could relocate the actual PCT.

But patience was not my forte in the snow. I habitually hurried in these situations. Snow, rocks, hurrying and very long legs are a recipe for getting bitch-slapped up against these rocks. I kept marking up my shins, while anxiously searching for the trail in the snows of the Sierra.

∗∗∗

It just didn't make any sense.

"Words cannot describe how bad the mosquitoes can be on the PCT," Yogi had written in her guidebook.

Some hikers practically bowed-up like pugilists when I asked about the bugs in the Sierras. *Why?* When the AT had reached higher elevations in New Hampshire and Maine, bugs had been completely absent. Now here we traveling consistently over 10,000 feet, and the bugs had people in virtually a state of shock.

But then it began to make perfect sense. The ubiquity of these bugs is a product of the clear snow melt. PCT hikers arrive in the Sierra Nevada in late June, right at the height of the melt. Consequently, we're greeted not just by roaring, crashing streams, but also by swarms of miniature, blood-sucking monsters.

Pat, Lauren, and I walked parallel to Woods Creek, with its white rapids tumbling towards us from the north. Very inspiring. Better yet, streams from all different directions seemed to be flowing into it. The story we had heard was that there were afternoons in the High Sierras in which you ford more streams than you do on the entire Appalachian Trail. This must have been one of those days. Quickly, I figured out it only made sense to keep my shoes and socks on, instead of changing them out each time.

Meanwhile, the bugs were agonizing and getting worse.

"These things intimidate me," I anguished. "You know why?"

"Because they're everywhere," Lauren said.

"Because they're so easy to kill,"

It was true. There was no sport to it at all. Someone told me that each bug lives a couple weeks. During that time they attack and blood-suck like there is no tomorrow. They just landed on your arms and put the straw to you. It was no problem to slap and kill them at any time. They seemed perfectly willing to accept death for just one last coveted drink of us.

Lush meadows and heavily bushy areas were the worst. We passed up some camp spots that were otherwise perfect. Finally, we made it to a rocky, promontory overlooking a creek. Although PCT regulations forbid camping within 100 feet of a water source, we camped there, thinking the open air might head off bugs. Hardly. I was only able to eat just a few bites while anxiously scurrying around, before practically diving into the safe haven of my tent.

***

CanaDoug didn't seem to harbor the anti-American resentments or chip-on-the-shoulder syndrome we so often see in our northern cousins. But, at the end of the day, he was a Canadian to the core.

"Do you want to share a room?" he had asked me back in Independence.

I had hesitated before finally answering, "Honestly, I've been looking forward to this night for eight days. I'm gonna' stay alone." A rare trace of unpleasantry had flashed across his face. Deciding to get a single room had seemed like just one more decision, amongst the countless decisions you face as a long-distance hiker. But my impression was that to CanaDoug, this was a breach of faith. Canadians are more communitarian than Americans. Perhaps I had violated some cultural taboo. Whatever the case, he hadn't been treating me the same way since.

Now, we were approaching Mather Pass together. As was our custom, he led and I followed. Since "the incident" in Independence he had instituted a new custom of blasting fart after fart right up at me. We were outdoors and they were harmless, to be sure. But it was done in a disrespectful way, as opposed to the usually playful hiker flatulence (Yes, I know this all sounds a bit esoteric!). He also had newly established his '500 foot rule'. For each increase of 500 feet in elevation he would stop, lay down, and take a cigar and food break. Of course, this was all completely his prerogative. But it only made sense to have a hiking partner getting through these snowy mountain passes in the Sierras. He knew this, and seemed like he was enjoying throwing me off balance a little bit.

"Wow." I said looking at the steep granite wall over to our left as we zeroed in on Mather Pass. "That had better not be it."

"We'll see," CanaDoug said.

The day before we had debriefed several southbounders coming off Mather Pass about what lay ahead for us.

"It's a bit gnarly," a couple of them had reported. The way they furrowed their brows worried me. I would soon come to hate this word, 'gnarly', even more than the word sketchy.

The trail turned right and I breathed a minor sigh of relief. But then to my consternation, the trail bent sharply left and we were headed straight at the granite wall. Mather Pass was on a shelf a few hundred feet above us. Between here and there were nothing but *rock scree* and snow.

"So this is what those assholes meant by gnarly, huh?" I angrily bitched. It was impossible to find the actual PCT. It was buried in the snow somewhere, but who knew where.

"We're gonna' have to go up," CanaDoug said.

"Where?" I asked anxiously. "That's much steeper than anything we've ever climbed."

"You've gotta' grab the scree and pull up using it."

"Man, this is dangerous as hell," I said anxiously.

"Just watch me," he said.

CanaDoug started grabbing rocks and hauling himself slowly up. I followed. It was steep and got steeper. It also was a lot longer climb than it had appeared from the bottom.

"Watch out, Skywalker," he said. "These rocks are loose."

Just like on Forrester's Pass, my anxiety got the best of me, and I kept hurrying right up to CanaDoug's heels.

"Watch it Skywalker, these rocks could fall. Get back."

"Yeah, yeah." I'd pull back, but not for long. It was impossible to stay calm on a hill this steep. The rock scree we were using as stepping stones weren't firm. It didn't take much imagination to conjure up a catastrophe scenario. Finally, CanaDoug got to the top. The very last ten feet were the most difficult for me.

"No, no, this way, Skywalker," he said.

I was plenty lucky right here. Since it was the last step I was able to take off my backpack and lob it up to the shelf, and then haul myself over.

"Good job," CanaDoug said.

"What do you reckon was the angle on that slope?" I asked. "Honestly?"

"Maybe 50 degrees," he answered.

Lauren came up last in an agonizingly slow ascent. Lauren was only 17 years-old with a Rebecca of Sunnybrook farm innocence about her. Unlike me, though, she was calm enough to take it slow and take breaks. Finally, after almost a half-hour of holding us in suspense, she pulled herself up. We had all gained Mather's Pass, where we looked down on another heavily snow-laden field laced with hiker footprints.

I sure was glad my Canadian hiking partner had put on his benevolent leader hat again. The high snows of the High Sierra had this lanky Georgia boy psyched out.

Chapter 23

Just a Survivor

Lauren and I (see first chapter) stood halfway down the north slope of snowy Muir Pass, trying to figure out how in the world to get out of here. It was the third of July.

"I'd give it a 60% chance the trail continues down through those lakes to the valley, a 30% chance it goes straight up these mountains, and a 10% chance it does neither," I told Lauren. Silence.

We had essentially narrowed our options down to two choices—climb the steep mountain ahead or descend through the lakes to the valley. The great problem is that at least one of these two options was drastically wrong and would lead to completely unforeseen consequences.

The high snows (summertime included) of the High Sierras were at turns laborious, exhilarating, terrifying.

"I doubt it goes up that mountain," she finally said.

"I tend to agree," I said. "But it did go over something just like that two days ago at Mather Pass."

I've been involved in the stock market most of my adult life. The cardinal rule is that when everybody agrees on something, they are almost always wrong. Hopefully, decision-making in the mountains would be different!

"Why don't we head down through the two lakes," I suggested.

"I think it might be on the left," she said.

"But remember back at Pinchot Pass," I countered. "The descent *slooked* through all those lakes."

"Yeah," Lauren said skeptically. "I think it might run to the left of the lakes."

"I don't see where," I said.

"I think I see it," she said evenly.

"Where?" I asked in disbelief.

"Yeah, look down where the snow runs out," she said. "Isn't that the PCT?" Sure enough a footpath that looked like the PCT ran along the bank of the left lake.

I had been gravely worried for the last several hours that we were seriously lost; so I was going to be the last person to realize we actually weren't lost. I hurriedly stumbled over rocks to get to the trail. "Yeah, this looks like it," I yelled back to Lauren, and rushed ahead. "And there's Pat."

"Who?" she yelled forward, jokingly.

"This way, this way," Pat started directing the two of us over yet another stream. "That rock, there, there." He was being unusually attentive. It had been about eight hours since he'd last seen his mapless hiking partner, Lauren. Perhaps, he was feeling guilty. If he was, he knew just the way to make it up.

The three of us hiked together to the banks of yet another gorgeous alpine lake. There Pat pulled out a fishing line he had been carrying in his monstrous backpack. Fifteen minutes later, he was back.

"Any luck?" I asked.

"Heck, yeah," he chortled. "I caught seven fish. Your line drops the minute you throw it in." We all went scavenging for wood and soon had us a roaring fire. Pat cooked the fish, wrapped them in tinfoil, and said, "Skywalker, you're first." He handed me two steaming fish.

"Oh, come on, I didn't do anything," I said.

Needless to say, it was just a pro-forma protest. I hadn't eaten anything hot in several days and was running low on food again. In comparison with hiker food, this tasted like the ambrosia of the gods.

I had never even been on an overnight hike until I was 44 years-old. It showed in my often erratic emotions. By contrast, I had started playing golf at age six. I instinctively knew that adversity was part of the game, and usually kept my cool no matter how I played. Maybe days like this would help me grow up as a hiker.

***

"Two cannibals are having lunch together," I said to *HWAP*. "One is complaining about the food. What does the other person respond?"

"Beats me," HWAP said.

"'Well then', he advises 'just push your ex-girlfriend over to the side of the plate and eat your vegetables.'"

HWAP gave the obligatory laugh which encouraged me to continue.

"Why don't cannibals eat divorcees?"

"Got me again," HWAP said.

"Because they taste so bitter."

Yeah, I know. But give me a break. Over the course of more than 2,600 miles anybody is bound to go cold for awhile. At least these lame, but morbid, jokes had a context. We were all running severely low on food.

Nobody had enough to get to the next town, Mammoth. So everybody was hoping to get to a resort called Vermillon Valley Resort (VVR). However, this required taking a side trail for two miles off the PCT, and then a catching the twice-a-day ferry to the resort. VVR offered a free first beer to hikers, before ripping us off on whatever items we needed for re-supply.

I had broken camp early and was hiking full speed, hoping to make the afternoon ferry. Surprisingly, I had run into HWAP. Surely the reader has already figured out that HWAP stands for Hooker With a Penis. It was obvious. Right? But in case it wasn't, you've got company. Honest to God, I must have asked him four times how the heck he ended up with that trail name. He patiently explained it every time, but I never really understood the derivation. All I know is that *Das Boots* (whose trail name derived from the German-looking jackboots he wore) gave it to him, and it stuck. Remember, we're out here a helluva' long time.

HWAP was in his mid-twenties and ex-military. Actually, he was such a strong hiker that I had never expected to see again. But he had come down with a severe case of *Giardia* (an intestinal disease from drinking contaminated water). Water treatment is always a bit of a roll of the dice. I had been so mesmerized by the rushing white-capped streams at the high elevations that I had just been sticking my bottle in and drinking up, without treating it with chemicals or filtering. So far, I had gotten away with it. However, HWAP had done the same and been laid low.

Because of the extra couple days it took him to get through the Sierras, his food supply was running dangerously low—some peanuts and raisins. I needed to make it to VVR today. He had to make it. We were moving pretty good, and as was usually the case when you haven't seen somebody you know for awhile, we were vigorously gossiping about what our colleagues were up to.

"I didn't think we had a climb here," I said surprised.

"Yeah, there's a climb," he said calmly.

It was a heckuva' climb. Next thing you know, we were scaling rock walls and jumping streams.

"Man, I've got doubts this is it."

"I'd be surprised if it wasn't," he said.

Unfortunately, I ended up being correct and we had to retrace the steep terrain we had just ascended. Now we were at risk of missing the ferry.

"Man, I'm really sorry," HWAP said.

And—even more impressive—he would later take responsibility for it in conversations in front of others.

For several straight miles we hiked all out to try to make it. Along the way, I did my first-ever *face-plant*—falling straight forward on my face. We arrived just in time, at which point I stumbled again rushing up the ramp of the ferry in front of a crowd of amazed onlookers. Perhaps it was a fitting end to my journey through the High Sierra. It wasn't pretty, but I made it.

But it doesn't capture the Sierras one bit. It's easy to over-romanticize something like this. Yet I have got to believe that the snow-capped peaks, rushing streams, lush green meadows, and sharp granite faces of the High Sierra put it in the category of one of the most beautiful places on the entire earth.

The idea of a gift to yourself sounds inherently narcissistic. I've never been much for birthday celebrations (ask some of my ex-girlfriends!). But by immersing myself so deeply in such indescribable beauty for the last few weeks, I honestly felt like I had given myself one of the great gifts of my forty-eight years.

Chapter 24

Three's Not the Charm

Bad things happen in threes. Right?

HWAP and I had spent a day re-supplying in Mammoth Mountain. Everything about this resort town had been new and cool. The roads, the post office, the free trolley system—it was all brand spanking new. The Great Recession never seemed to have even happened in these gold-plated environs.

HWAP and I were on the the bus going back to the PCT at Red's Meadow, when I suddenly blurted out, "Oh, shit."

"What?" he said calmly.

I began frantically rifling through my backpack.

" %#* dammit, I left my tent poles in the room," I steamed.

Apparently—at least in HWAP's later recounting of the scene to other hikers—the entire bus had gone hush over this giant's (my) temper tantrum.

"This stop," I yelled out to the driver.

"I'll wait for you at Red's Meadow," HWAP said.

"No, just keep going," I said, realizing how bad I'd screwed up. "I'll try to catch up with you in Yosemite."

HWAP had been the ideal hiking partner, and I hated getting separated from him like this. In fact, it was to be the last time I ever saw him. I flagged down a car that was going down the mountain. "Stop here, please." I then practically announced to the elderly couple in the car they were going to give me a ride. They took me back to the motel where I went into chicken-with- my-head-cut-off mode. The front desk clerk gave me a key to the room, but the tent poles weren't there.

I rushed back to the front desk, and said, "The maid must have thrown 'em away. Can I look in the dumpster?" They assigned a Mexican maid to take me out to the dumpster, where I frantically rummaged through garbage without luck. *I'm screwed. No way I can find a two-person tent long enough for me in this town.*

"Who cleaned the room?" I peppered the people at the front desk. They all concerned themselves with trying to sort the problem out.

The more cynical reader might just have become suspicious the problem lay elsewhere. I became suspicious of that possibility, too. I hurriedly dug deep into my backpack. Of course, angled off to the side of my backpack were the bloody tent poles.

***

Particularly strange things can happen at high elevations.

I had run into CanaDoug leaving Mammoth the second time.

"Where's HWAP?" he asked.

After I coughed up the embarrassing explanation, he said, "Don't worry. We should make it to Yosemite by tomorrow night." Indeed, we hiked until dark and got off early the next morning.

"I'll catch right up," I said to CanaDoug as he headed off. "I'm going to dry my tent off."

I began flailing the tent in every direction to wick any moisture off it. *Whap.* One of the tent straps hit my finger and opened a crease. Blood began flowing freely. I anxiously rifled through my first aid packet, and tried applying band-aids. But the blood kept oozing. My fingers were biting cold up here above 10,000 feet.

Why won't it quit bleeding? I began to suspect it had something to do with the high altitude. I also began to panic. There had been a couple unexplained deaths on the PCT in 2006. One guy apparently had a heart attack and was found in the middle of the trail. The other was found down a steep hill where he had fallen. *But wouldn't this be the freakiest death ever—bleeding to death on the trail from a minor cut?*

I had no idea what to do. Finally, being a creature of hope, I

If nature is your thing, the PCT is tough to beat.

just decided to hike forward and hope like heck to find somebody with some bandages. I kept the bleeding finger in my little towel, but it kept gushing and turned the towel a shock of red. Finally, I spotted a family camped up the hill and approached them.

"Excuse me," I said. "Do you have any wrapping tape. I'm losing a lot of blood."

It was a family of Mexicans and my question was greeted with blank stares. So I repeated it in a brand of spanish that Forrest Gump would be extremely proud of, and held out my pouring red finger for emphasis.

"You need pressure," he said, and pulled out some gauze pads and tape and wrapped it brilliantly.

"Wow, do you have medical training?"

"No, but blood no stop at high elevations."

"Golly, I can't thank you enough," I said. "I don't need all the food I'm carrying. Please let me share it."

"No thank you, mister," his wife responded. "You want hot burrito."

Needless to say, I craved the possibility of a hot burrito. But this guy conceivably had just saved my life.

"No thanks," I lied. "I just ate a big breakfast."

Off I went trying to make up for lost time.

I proceeded to lose a helluva' lot more, walking for miles along shimmering Thousand Island Lake, thinking of my good luck and the beautiful scenery. I wasn't seeing any footprints. Usually, when I was worried about being lost, I was just being over-vigilant. But this trail was a talisman. It was well-maintained enough in various places to keep suckering me along. I followed it for miles along this massive lake. Finally, it just completely gave out. All I could do is angrily retrace my steps for over three miles. Now it was going to require 29 miles, instead of twenty-two to reach Yosemite National Park today. But given everything I'd always heard about Yosemite, I really wanted to get there.

Donahue Pass lay between here and there. Worst of all, someone had described it with that god-awful word, 'sketchy'. Fortunately, it didn't rise to the level of sketchiness—or even gnarliness—that some of its kin had. Now it was a matter of gliding at my maximum speed of perhaps a little over three miles- per-hour along the gorgeous Tuolomne River, which flowed the entire way to Yosemite. My amateur outdoorsman's eye was able to notice that the deer in the meadow on the other side of the river stayed out in the middle of the pasture. Undoubtedly, that was to give them good sight lines for where their attackers (bears and wolves) habitually emerged from late in the day.

Finally, I took the side turn directing me to the well-known Tuolomne Meadows Campground. Parked campers and throngs of tourists filled every nook and cranny of this monstruous playground. It was a scene straight out of *Americana*. And I was licking my chops.

Let me just say this. Plenty of these road trippers were surely better versed in outdoor matters than this here hiker. But in one area, they were no match for any long-distance hiker. Food.

Ninety-nine percent of road-trippers pack 200% or more of the food they need. Long-distance hikers have a very different philosophy. And the longer the distances you cover, the closer you learn to cut it. I never met a hiker who wasn't a total opportunist. Give him or her any opening, and they will make Robin Hood proud in redistributing food from those who have lots of it, to those who devour lots of it. I was no slouch at this myself.

I wandered through the Tuolomne Meadows Campground attracting various stares. Finally, I got the question I was waiting for. "Gosh, you must have a big advantage with those long legs?" some lady asked nicely. "Just how tall are you?"

Two delicious hamburgers and some vegetables and blueberry pie later, she and her family had all the answers.

"You can stay right here with us," the family offered.

However, I wanted to find my colleagues somewhere in the campground.

"Well, we're having a big breakfast, please come back."

"Oh please, now," I joked.

But I just managed to stumble down there and run into them again the next morning, where ample helpings of pancakes, bacon, and eggs greeted me. Yeah, folks. Life sure is hell on the PCT.

It was dark, but I thought I spotted Ingrid in the distance.

"Ingrid, is that you?"

"Skywalker," she yelled back."

"Is there anywhere I can camp here?" I said.

"Yes, right there," she said. "And you can lock your food up in the locker here."

"Where's the rest of *Team Hustle* (Dirk, Laura, and Snake Charmer)?"

"Team Hustle has broken up," she said in a downcast fashion.

"What happened?"

"Laura and Snake Charmer went back to his house in Los Angeles for a week. Dirk is meeting up with his girlfriend."

"Do you think they'll come back?" I asked Ingrid (I knew Dirk would).

"I don't know. Their feet are hurting pretty badly."

Snake Charmer and Laura had met at the Kickoff and hiked every step of the way. In fact, in what would be the culmination of their PCT romance, they even got MRI's on their feet together. Then they quit together. Shades of *Romeo and Juliet*, but with a much less tragic ending.

Ingrid and I stood there chatting about the sights in Yosemite when we heard loud screams, followed by banging of pots and pans. There was only one possible explanation.

"That's probably a bear," said Ingrid, the former   student park ranger. We heard more people yelling "bear". Apparently, it was moving our way. I stood there watching over Ingrid's right shoulder looking for the bear to appear. The gentlemanly thing to do was not to impede her view of the bear, by standing between the bear and her. *Right*? *Right*?

"Where is it?" I asked.

"Over there somewhere," Ingrid said.

Finally, somebody's flashlight shined on a medium-sized bear strolling through the campground like an insolent teenager.

His or her attitude seemed to be *"You're all a pain in the ass. And I know you're not going to shoot me. So just shut up and let me see what damn food is lying around."*

Soon an armed ranger came up trying to shoo the bear away. Alas, this may have been one of this bear's last passes through this campground. The next morning somebody told us he had seen two tags on the bear. That meant it had been anesthetized and moved from the area twice, but kept coming back. The policy is 'three strikes and you're out'.

This was a fitting end to an eventful day. I was in high spirits because tomorrow I was taking a bus down into Yosemite Valley to get a tour of *Nature's Cathedral.*

It had been the life mission of one most extraordinary man to preserve it for us masses to enjoy.

Chapter 25

Scottish-American Beacon

I care to live only to entice people to look at Nature's loveliness.

John Muir

On the streets of Dunbar, Scotland, thousands of miles from where he would later achieve fame, it was evident early on that John Muir was different. The popular Scottish poet, Robert Burns, was the most decisive influence on his youth.

"On my lonely walks I have often thought how fine it would be to have the company of Burns," Muir wrote. "Wherever a Scotsman goes, there goes Burns."

Like so many Scots, Burns had a burning sense of social inferiority. Defiantly, he refused to use the imperial English language— the language of conquest. Burns wrote such classics as *Auld Lang Syne , Tam O' Shanter*, and *Sweet Afton* in the old Scots dialect.

The Scots revered Burns as a national hero. His poetry, along with other Scottish poets, including Robert Louis Stevenson and Walter Scott, would inspire John Muir for the rest of his life in his fight on behalf of underdog causes.

***

"This sudden splash into pure wildness," John Muir exulted, "How utterly happy it has made us. Oh, that glorious Wisconsin wilderness."

In 1848, Muir's father had uprooted the family from Scotland, due to a dispute with the Church of Scotland. Nothing was more important to a Scot than land, given their bitter experience with imperial English landlords. Because Daniel Muir had saved up enough money in thrifty Scottish fashion, he was able to purchase 300 acres of Wisconsin farmland.

John was eleven at the time of that first American summer, and slept outside most of the time in order to fully imbibe the pristine wilderness. The amazing array of wildlife—squirrels, frogs, turtles, bears, rabbits—left him positively rhapsodic. The biggest cloud on the horizon, he would later recall, was that he soon joined all the other American boys in carrying a rifle. Like everyone, he killed animals in scores.

But John Muir was different than most red-blooded American boys. Soon he recoiled from this practice. In fact, he thought the whole practice had revealed a dark side of human nature.

"Why should man value himself as more than a small part of creation?" he asked. "Every species has been made in the same way as humans." Using alligators as an example, he even went so far as to reason that because they have a right to live, they have a right to eat whatever they catch. This would include an occasional human!

"If a war of races should occur between the wild beasts and Lord Man," he wrote, "I would be tempted to sympathize with the bears."

Muir's father was a stern Calvinist, and often set up piles of burning brush on the farm, signifying hellfire and brimstone. Beatings soon followed. Ultimately, his father's harshness towards both himself and the farm animals drove Muir away from the farm. He enrolled at the University of Wisconsin in Madison where he soon faced another major moral crisis. The Civil War broke out. Muir considered himself a Scot, first and foremost. More importantly, he didn't believe in killing humans any more than animals. So he took the time-honored route of pacifists and headed to Canada.

After the war, Muir decided to travel the length of the country. Quickly, he developed his trademark style. He traveled on foot, carrying a loaf of bread and tea. When his loaf gave out he was known to occasionally knock on people's doors asking for a loaf of bread in return for giving a hand at chores. Often he went hungry. But he never worried. Nature, he assumed, could never harm him, for it was the fundamental source of all health. Sickness was something that belonged to the cities.

During his extensive wanderings, Muir began hearing about a place called *Yosemite* in California. Quickly, he resolved to seek this paradise out. California would prove to lay such a deep hold on his affections that he would never again live anyplace else.

***

When Muir arrived in San Francisco in 1868, he allegedly asked the first passer-by how he could quickly get out of town. Asked where he was going, Muir simply said, "any place that is wild." The trail led across the Bay and eventually into the Sierras.

Ecstatic is the only way to describe Muir when he first spotted the dark-green forest and smooth, unbroken walls of granite peaks. His first summer in the Sierras awakened the deepest and most intense passion of his life. His whole body seemed to pulse with the beauty around him.

"This splendid country," he wrote, "flowing with more of milk and more of honey than did old Canaan in its happiest prime."

Muir thought nature—especially mountains—actually led humans to goodness and light.

"I am hopelessly and forever a mountaineer," he exulted.

Californians who witnessed Muir wandering around the Sierras marveled at the risks he took. Muir simply couldn't get enough. On a later trip to Alaska, he and his dog had gotten stuck on the massive Taylor glacier, and made a harrowing escape. Telling of the dog's bravery jumping over crevasses became one of his famous tales.

Not everyone was enchanted, though.

He "knows less about camping than almost any man I've ever

camped with," remarked an amazed member of one of Muir's far-flung expeditions.

He often set off deep into the back country with insufficient gear, and went long stretches with no food. He could easily have died from hypothermia or a fall off one of the precipices he constantly sought out. But Muir trusted so deeply in the benevolence of nature that he simply didn't worry.

***

California's population exploded upon completion of the Trans-Continental Railroad in 1869. Far-reaching decisions about the American West quickly moved to the forefront. Muir's outdoor exploits had already made him legendary, which allowed him middle of the fierce debates.

He bought a house in San Francisco. In Donald Worster's brilliant biography of Muir, *A Passion for Nature*, he points out that Muir was actually embarrassed at this bow to civilization. In fact, when greeting visitors he always tried to give the impression that he had just returned from the mountains. But it was a necessary evil, and gave him a larger platform. Better yet, unlike Thoreau who preferred to live in monastic-like solitude (Walden Pond), Muir was a people person who could win over almost anybody.

Great moment in American wilderness preservation. John Muir and Theodore Roosevelt posing at Glacier Point with Yosemite Falls in the background. No offense, Mr. President, but my vote goes to the dapper gentleman to your left!

One of those in the thrall of the Muir legend was the 26th President of the United States, Theodore Roosevelt. Roosevelt fancied himself an outdoorsman par excellence, and figured Muir to be a kindred soul.

When planning his tour of the West in 1903 he wrote Muir a letter asking for a tour of Yosemite.

"I do not want anyone with me but you," Roosevelt wrote him.

Upon arrival, President Roosevelt gave all the other gathered dignitaries short shrift, and shunted the Secret Service aside. Thus set off together two of the great raconteurs of all time, as well as seminal figures in American outdoor history. They would be together for three days and three nights. Needless to say, Muir knew exactly where to take him. They hiked to and camped in the most beautiful spots in Yosemite, including at the foot of Bridal Veil Falls with its fantastic view of El Capitan and Ribbon Falls gushing down from the valley's north rim.

Muir proved masterful at stoking up Roosevelt's wilderness fervor, filling him with one tale after another of reckless timber cutting. Soon he had Roosevelt shouting "swine" at these villains.

"I stuffed him pretty well regarding the timber thieves," Muir fondly recalled.

Now he sought to get Roosevelt to add the scenic wonders in Yosemite Valley to the already federally-protected Yosemite National Park. Roosevelt heartily agreed and proved good to his word.

The only sour point in this veritable love-fest came one night around a campfire when the 44 year-old Roosevelt uncorked his colorful array of tales of big-game hunting. The 65 year-old Muir couldn't resist himself.

"Mr. Roosevelt," he asked, "when are you going to get beyond the boyishness of killing things?"

Roosevelt was temporarily taken aback, but finally responded in an uncharacteristically soft manner. "Muir, I guess you are right." However, Roosevelt never gave up hunting big game.

Their three days in Yosemite rated as a highlight in both of their lives, and both would speak glowingly of the other (Muir—"I fairly fell in love with him.") for the rest of their lives. Unfortunately though, his greatest defeat would follow on the heels of it.

***

The flowering of interest in wilderness preservation was now to run into the great reality of the West—the scarcity of water. San Francisco was growing into a world-class city and needed more water. The city set its periscope on Hetch-Hetchy Valley, which lay 150 miles away *inside* Yosemite National Park. This valley, with its scenic waterfalls and surrounding mountains, also happened to be one of John Muir's favorite places.

He was horrified when he heard what was afoot.

"These devotees of raging commercialism," he fumed. "They're temple destroyers."

However, Gifford Pinchot, who was Theodore Roosevelt's point man in these matters, proclaimed a wise-use doctrine. The water should be used in the way to benefit the most people. It came down to the most basic philosophy. Pinchot thought allowing San Francisco to have the water was the best possible use for the most number of people. Muir, with his absolute faith in Nature, thought keeping the valley pristine offered the most long-term benefits for the most number of people.

It is impossible to conclusively say who was conceptually right. Pinchot probably had the best argument for the next century—Muir for the millenia. Objectively, though, Muir was making his argument at the wrong time and in the wrong country. Theodore Roosevelt listened sympathetically to Muir's pleadings to stop this abomination of nature. But ultimately Roosevelt was influenced by the fact that the United States had just passed the European powers to become the world's largest economy. Roosevelt didn't want anything to derail the nation's industrial might and chose not to intervene to save the Hetch-Hetchy Valley from being dammed.

It was a bitter defeat for Muir and one he never recovered from his remaining few years.

***

The famous diplomat and historian, Henry Kissinger, is fond of saying, "Ultimately, a person's place in history is determined as much by what he set in motion, as by what he actually accomplished." His formula could well apply to John Muir.

Muir helped found the Sierra Club in 1892, which now has a membership totaling almost a million members. Most importantly, an entire culture dedicated to preserving wilderness has reached critical mass. Its best days are likely yet to come because it is so wildly popular amongst our youth.

Nobody has ever played a bigger role in that movement than the gentleman with the longish gray beard, merry blue eyes, an inimitable Scottish accent, and the pose of an Old Testament Prophet. John Muir probably rates as the greatest proponent of Nature in American history.

Chapter 26

"Worst Bug Day in PCT History"

Never kill a mosquito or blackfly. If you do, a million other ones will come to its funeral.

Verlen Kruger

If you had asked me in the desert what was the most important piece of equipment in my backpack, I might have said my wide-brimmed sun hat. In the High Sierra, I would have dithered before possibly answering my long-johns. But for the next 100 miles through Yosemite, there was no doubt, whatsoever, what was the most critical item. It was a piece of equipment that probably weighed about 1/100th of a pound. My headnet.

Yogi had recommended carrying a headnet in her guidebook, but it had almost seemed gimmicky to me. Obviously, you couldn't keep it on while eating, drinking, defecating, or hiking. So why carry one? Right? Wrong. Fortunately, Dirk had deftly negotiated one for me in the desert from a section hiker who was ending his hike.

Yosemite National Park is an unbelievable world of sheer rock cliffs and running, plunging water. The sheer beauty of it is staggering. I had toured the Yosemite Valley the previous day and been blown away by the sights I had heard about all my life, including *El Capitan* and *Half-Dome*. Waterfalls were everywhere, including Yosemite Falls, which drops off 2,425 feet, the highest waterfall in North America.

Rushing streams are one of the major reasons I love hiking. Along with everything else, their power to clear the mind better is incomparable. But they come with a price, at least at certain times of the year. This was one of those times. The next five days going north out of Tuolomne, the bugs were to be hellish. It almost felt like a hot needle was being injected, every time one of them bit me. At first, I wore the headnet only on breaks. I would lift it up to take bites of food, and then quickly lower the veil to chew the food. Soon, though, it became obvious I was going to have to wear the headnet while hiking.

Relieving myself, however, proved to be terribly complicated. Twice *my unit* got bit while urinating. In both cases, it took a couple days of triple-antibiotic treatment for the wound and pain to go away. I took to frantically fanning everywhere when taking a leak, but wasn't confident in the technique.

"We're lucky to not have outdoor plumbing," one Canadian girl chortled, when other male hikers complained about having suffered the same fate.

The women didn't have a free ride by any imagination. They had to expose their full behinds to attack several times a day. I didn't envy them. But I sure admired the way some improvised. They learned to squat with their backpacks attached and get the job done quickly. I had never seen that before.

"You should put that technique on the internet," I sincerely suggested to a couple of them. It almost matched us males in its efficiency.

The challenge was psychological as much as physical. It was impossible to relax, knowing these bloodsuckers were savoring every moment.

"You look dazed," CanaDoug observed one day to me. "You've got cuts everywhere." He was an unabashed defender of Canada's geography, periodically mentioning this or that great mountain or water source as being equal or superior to the one in America. But he finally had to admit, "Yeah, these bugs are probably worse than anything I've ever seen." Plenty of hikers' shirts looked like they were changing to a darker color from all the dead bugs smeared on them.

The second night into Yosemite, CanaDoug, Ingrid, and I hiked until arriving on a sandy beach surrounding yet another large lake. *What in the world is a beach doing here in the middle of the mountains?* It was a total anomaly, but also gorgeous. Indeed, the Sierras doled out endless delights. But the hardships were formidable. Here on the sandy shores, the wind was overwhelming and I had to quickly take umbrage in my tent. But when it had died down the next morning, the bugs quickly smelled blood. It was unbearable and I literally had to run of there.

One rushing stream and amazing view after another presented themselves here in Nature's Cathedral. Amazingly, the bugs got even worse. Often, I would feel an ecstatic bug trilling in my ears, presumably to get at the wax inside. Instead of looking forward to breaks, I was now dreading them. But you had to have them. The three of us took a break at Kerrick Canyon before a big climb that lay ahead. But I quickly jumped up.

"I can't stand it," I said in a state of angst, and rushed off ahead of them. *A higher elevation should bring relief.*

Forget it. At the top, I came to a fork in the trail. Stopping to check my maps would have meant Chinese torture treatment from these invisible terrorists. So I just went straight. I headed up a mountain for two miles before the trail became ragged, and I realized I was lost. Dispirited and anxious, I hurriedly retraced my steps. Worst of all, once I found the PCT again, the trail led down to Dorothy Lake. There, all wind and all life appeared to have ceased—except for, of course, mosquitoes.

I had only a half hour of light left and hiked as fast as I possibly could, hoping to get to somewhere with at least a whiff of a humane breeze. I barely found it. After fording yet another creek, I quickly threw up my tent right in the middle of a fork in the trail, and buried myself inside. CanaDoug and Ingrid never arrived. Doug must have been at least a little shaky, himself. He would end up taking the wrong turn at this fork the next day and hike off course for several miles. That was especially unfortunate because it was to be the very worst bug day yet.

***

It was a little bit weird. I had a long-standing habit of talking to almost all south-bounders. It had served me well in the past. On this mid-July day I would see them coming a couple hundred yards away, looking like widows at a Catholic funeral.

I'd ask complete strangers through my net, "Are the bugs any better up ahead?"

"No," this one lady in her mid-thirties who appeared out of breath told me through her net. "In Grace Meadows I had to run, they were so tortuous."

That was discouraging, but believable. Unfortunately, I was absolutely forced to stop and defecate. But in the middle of it I had to go sprinting, the sharp bites on my non-DEET-treated rear-end were so acute.

Grace Meadows was another gorgeous grassy meadow, the product of over a hundred inches of precipitation per year. I would have probably stopped and had a prolonged picnic right here. But a break was now completely out of the question. Instead, it turned into a forced march, and a bit eerie of one at that. The thought kept recurring that the bugs were on a virtually equal footing with me. Finally, I got to Kennedy Canyon Creek where I called it a day.

Ingrid arrived, sans CanaDoug, just before dark.

"How was your day?" I asked.

A German's style is bound to be different from a southerner's style. The former are more empirical and understated. The latter are more prone to hyperbole.

"Worst bug day in PCT history," she stated without hesitation. This southerner couldn't have said it any better.

Chapter 27

The 'Root Canal' Aspect of Hiking

People who don't climb mountains tend to assume that the sport is a reckless, Dionysian pursuit of ever escalating thrills. But the notion that climbers are merely adrenaline junkies chasing a fix is a fallacy. It is a Calvinist undertaking.

Jon Krakauer *Into Thin Air*

Mountain climbing clearly is more dangerous than long-distance hiking by an order of great magnitude. But they do have a few things in common. Both begin with an initial frisson of excitement. Then, reality intrudes, and it becomes hard work.

To be sure, hiking trails attract their share of adrenaline junkies. Both the desert and the High Sierra had offered great novelty. But now we were entering a new phase that I frequently referred to as "the root canal aspect of thru-hiking." The ratio of pleasure to misery was bound to be unfavorable at times.

Long-distance hiking can feel like a job and not that easy of one—easily 70 hours a week and quite physically demanding. Why do it? Many chose not to. The trail would claim the forfeit of many hikers in northern California. Many of the dropouts were quite surprising. Of course, some were for reasons of legitimate injury. More often, though, the reason given was, "I'm not having fun anymore." Needless to say, that is a perfectly suitable excuse on the face of it. But if you looked deeper you saw nuance at work.

Strange as it sounds, many would quit at the top of their game. They would hike fast and furiously (25 or 30 mile days), hurrying to a trail town. When they arrived the adrenaline would be rushing. There, great festivities would ensue. The hiker would almost always be talking along the lines of, "I'm heading back out tomorrow to go long." But then the *tyranny of civilization* would take over. They wouldn't want to leave town.

In one sense, it was a thing of beauty watching hikers dissect these backwater trail towns in such efficient fashion. Everybody would be scurrying around on a shoestring ("The post office is down there." "The Laundromat is behind that building." "Have you seen the grocery store?" "No, any idea where the outfitter and the internet are?"). It was much more mentally taxing than a day on the trail, and just as important. In a matter of hours, we routinely prepared for trips that would take most people weeks or even months to map out and provision.

Even the hikers disciplined enough to leave town on schedule would have palpably more downbeat looks on their faces than when arriving in town. Perhaps the moral of the story is that as uncivilized as we humans so often act, we are ultimately civilized beings. The sad thing is that so many of the people who got off the trail in this fashion would have been perfectly happy if they could have just forced themselves to hoist their pack, hitch back to the trail, and take the very first few steps. The challenge simply lay in beginning.

In his bestselling book, *A Walk in the Woods*, Bill Bryson spoke of the 'low-level ecstasy'—so scarce in American life—that he found while hiking. I, too, retained bedrock faith that long- distance hiking was an endeavor utterly anathema to false gods, such as celebrity and money worship. Thus, it was an extremely healthy thing to do.

I had a demanding challenge ahead to make it to Canada. And it was going to be all the more difficult due to a factor that was beginning to loom larger by the day.

***

The average height of the Boston Marathon winner in the 20th century was just over 5' 7". An entire century is too long for the statistic to be a fluke. Likewise, if you look at the podium for decathlon events, you will see it disproportionately weighted towards people on the short side. In other words, being short is an advantage in endurance events.

On a normal day, a hiker of average height with an average weight backpack would use approximately 5,000 calories. However, I probably used closer to 7,000 calories per day. For a typical five day journey from one trail town to the next, over 30,000 calories were required for me to break even. I usually carried about half of that. I don't need to tell you the results. After 1,000 miles I was down 30 pounds, with over 1,600 miles to travel. And I was absolutely bankrupt for ideas as to how to staunch this hemorrhaging of weight.

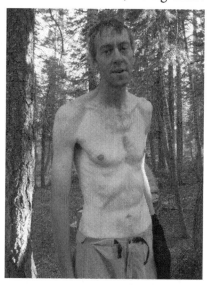

"That's scary," Poet immediately said, when she saw my emaciated upper body. Indeed, crushing weight loss and fatigue made me vastly more sensitive to the nighttime cold.

In trail towns, I would call my mother up and anguish over this problem.

"Bill, listen to me." she would sternly lecture me. "You've got to carry more food."

"My backpack already weighs a lot more than on the Appalachian Trail," I would shoot back. "The more weight I carry, the more calories I use up." It was all a downward spiral.

The only surefire way to break it was to hike less miles per day. However, for the first time I was beginning to hear that *ticking sound*. It was imperative that I begin to hike more miles on a daily basis if I was to make it to Canada. And I badly wanted to make it.

Chapter 28

Alone

Someone—somewhere—pointed out that if you are miserable when you're alone, then the problem is that you are keeping bad company. I had hiked in the midst of the bubble of hikers most of the way. Now, though I was going to be alone a lot.

CanaDoug's motto was moderation. He took great Canadian pride that he could handle whatever cold weather the hiking gods threw at him in October in northern Washington. So he was in no real hurry. But I was.

In a way, I was looking forward to it. Now, I would see what I was capable of. The gold standard on the Appalachian Trail had been 20 mile days. However, on the PCT, once out of the Sierra Nevada Mountains, the gold standard becomes 25 miles per day. It required discipline for me to hike 25 miles in one day. Objectively, though, that was one of my strengths as a hiker.

Typically, I would get up soon after first light. It always maddened me that I couldn't get off faster. There were just too many things to do—gather everything up and put in the right stuff sack, treat my feet with ointment, eat a cold breakfast, break down the tent, head off to the bushes to perform ablutions, and usually retrieve water from any nearby source. I rarely could get all this done in less than an hour; but never gave up looking for ways to reduce it.

It normally took me right about 12 or 13 hours to hike 25 miles. My walking speed probably averaged about 2.6 miles per hour, depending on the terrain and topography. This left room for a five minute break every hour during which I typically devoured a snickers or granola bar. Also, I would try to take a lunch break of at least an hour in the early afternoon. This was usually a packet of tuna, bites out of a block of cheese, triscuits and bagels and peanut butter, and beef jerky. Usually, around 8:30 I would actively begin scouting for a flat place to put my tent. Unfortunately, dinner looked a helluva' lot like breakfast and lunch.

In *A Blistered Kind of Love*, Angela and Duffy Ballard referred to the intense solitude of long-distance hiking as *spectacular monotony*. Whatever oscillations a hiker has in morale throughout the day, the primary trend is almost always upward to some state of grace—or call it low-level ecstasy—by the time one sets up camp.

***

I can't resist saying it, again. You've just got to see this PCT. It can actually stagger you with its sheer beauty.

In South Lake Tahoe, I had performed what has become a rite of passage for PCT hikers by committing an atrocity at the buffet at Harrah's. Obviously, this wasn't a panacea to my weight hemorrhaging problem. But at least it made me feel like I was trying something.

The trail out of Tahoe had followed gorgeous Echo Lake for miles before coming to an even more beautiful body of water, Aloha Lake. Glaciers have carved the rocky soil to give this sub-alpine region an alpine setting. Stunning granite cliff-like peaks with white snow caps tower above the shoreline of white rocks, making this perhaps the most underrated view on the entire PCT.

Often, it is the unexpected views that have the strongest impact. Or at least that's my excuse for why I got lost for the fourth time in the last two weeks. Soon I was all the way on the far side of Aloha Lake. That was confusing because, according to my data book, I was supposed to be climbing by now. Finally, I did start precipitously winding up some steep mountain. Then, I got a break.

The only person I would see the next several hours was an

older fella' who came piking down this mysterious mountain I was now climbing. Better yet, he was a veteran local hiker.

"Excuse me sir," I addressed him anxiously. "Is this the PCT?"

"I don't think so," he said softly.

"You don't think it is, or you know it's not?"

"It's not the PCT."

"Oh wow. Now I've got to go back a couple miles, huh?"

"Not necessarily," he said. He then pulled out his maps and showed me a route over Mosquito Pass, followed by a labrynthine course that would put me back on the PCT in twelve miles.

An overpowering bright sun was bearing down on these white granite rocks. My high mileage goals for the day were in jeopardy, plus I wondered where I might find water if I needed it. For once, I decided to try to navigate my way back onto the PCT, instead of just putting my head between my tail and retracing my steps.

Let me say this about the Mosquito Pass trail I now doggedly pursued. When President Obama shuts down Guantanamo, they should consider transferring the prisoners here. They'd soon be begging to go back to Guantanamo. Mosquito Pass was a bug-ridden swampland.

Twice I came to turns in the trail that the man had not advised me about. All I could rationalize was that the PCT was somewhere to the east so I should probably take the right fork. Taking a break was completely out of the question given the ferocity of the mosquito attacks. Finally, I started scaling up a mountain per this man's instructions. After about 1,500 feet in elevation gain, I came upon a PCT sign. All's well that ends well, and my morale, so shaky for the last several hours, jumped.

Apparently the route had been a shortcut because Boo-Boo and D-Wreck, two hikers that had gone ahead of me that morning, soon came by with looks of total confusion.

"What took ya'll so long?" I kidded them.

"Did you parachute in?" D-Wreck asked befuddled.

I cut my break short just to be able to follow them. We got to Phipps Creek where the water flowed grudgingly, but the mosquitoes attacked with an agonizing ferocity. But we all needed water, and dutifully pulled out our filters.

"Hurry up or I'm setting the tent up," Boo-Boo commanded D-Wreck.

The God's honest truth is the mosquitoes were so tortuous that I had to put on my marmot jacket just to fill up one nalgene bottle of water.

Boo-Boo and D-Wreck hightailed it out of there, while I still pumped. I came upon them in a couple miles where they lay inside the protective netting of their tent. They didn't leave their tent and all I heard was discussion of how many more miles they would do tomorrow and the day after and so on. All about miles.

I lay there in my tent listening to the frequent sound of bugs' sorties colliding against my tent netting in their attempts to get at me.

***

Fortunately, I had the blue majesty of Lake Tahoe to keep me company for a little while. Actually, it was for more than a little while, given that Lake Tahoe is the largest alpine lake in North America with a circumference of 71 miles around. Up until now, most of the lakes we had passed were from glacier melt. But Lake Tahoe—the second deepest lake in America at 1,645 feet—is the product of a volcano explosion.

"I thought it must surely be the fairest picture the whole earth affords," Mark Twain wrote of the beautiful lake. Its tranquil presence is the ultimate in dreamlike serenity. Speaking of dreams, everybody should be afforded a few of those over the course of a Mexico-Canada journey on foot. Right? Here's mine.

All through the wonders of the High Sierra, and now following a rim above Lake Tahoe, I had a recurring thought. If Osama Bin Laden, Saddam Hussein, and George W. Bush could have gone on a backpacking trip together through this kind of hushed landscape, would they have been able to work out their differences in a less violent fashion? Obviously, it's a pie-in-the-sky scenario. But there is something about backpacking that brings out the better angels of our nature, as compared to politics and power.

Unfortunately, Lake Tahoe may not have the hold on backpackers that it once did. Besides its size, it is renowned for its crystal clear, blue water. But studies show it is up much less clear than just thirty years ago, due to over-construction and the consequent soil erosion mucking up the whole scene. It doesn't take a frothing-at-the-mouth eco-warrior to get bent out of shape over that.

***

I was intensely lonely and happy to run into Wisconsin and Firefly on the ridge overlooking Squaw Valley. A different kettle of fish they were. Wisconsin was essentially an anarchist.

"I hate money," he repeatedly said. "Look at how well we all get along out here trading things, bartering everything. Why can't the rest of the world be that way?"

His girlfriend, Firefly, was a professional roller-derby player and a real physical specimen, but with an amazingly elegant personality to match.

At our campsite overlooking Sherrold Lake, he pulled out some electrical device that was presumably compliments of the capitalist system he so detested.

"What songs would you like to hear, Skywalker?" he asked me.

"Have you got the Allman Brothers on there?" I asked.

"Yeah."

"How about *Midnight Rider*?"

The Allman Brothers were from my hometown of Macon, Georgia, so requesting this song was a small lapse into provincialism. In 1972, the group's guitarist, Duane Allman, had died when his motorcycle had crashed into the back of a peach truck. They subsequently named the album they had been working on, *Eat A Peach*. Its memorable lyrics, which came pouring out of Wisconsin's machine at 9,000 feet in the California mountains, go as follows:

> *Well, I've got to run to keep from hiding And*
> *I'm bound to keep on riding*
> *And I've got one more silver dollar*

But I'm not gonna' let 'em catch me, no Not
gonna' let 'em catch the midnight rider.

The song is a paen to freedom and independence, which, come to think about it, is kinda' what the PCT is. And the God's-honest-truth is that for the next two days this song carried me a total of fifty miles in an elevated state of morale.

Chapter 29

Donner's (Dahmer's) Pass

In the early spring of 1846, an advertisement appeared in the Springfield, Illinois Gazette.

"Westward ho," it declared. "Who wants to go to California without it costing them anything?" It sought eight able-bodied men. The ad was placed by 65 year-old George S. Donner. Like many farmers of the time, Donner craved more land in the West. Given the pioneer spirit of the mid-nineteenth century, this expedition soon swelled to 87 people.

Timing was everything. The wagon trains couldn't leave before the winter rains and snow stopped, yet it was absolutely crucial to clear the Sierra Nevada Mountains before the first heavy snows of the new season. On October 31, 1846 the Donner Party only needed to ascend a 1,000 more feet to have cleared the last mountain pass in the Sierras. At that point, it would be all downhill to their destination. The exhausted party raced up the pass. But heavy snow began to fall. By morning the pass had become completely blocked with twenty-foot snowdrifts. They had arrived one day too late. Thus commenced one of the most gruesome tales to ever unfold in the mountains.

Over the next four months, the men, women, and children huddled together in tents and make shift lean-tos. First, the cattle and dogs were all eaten. Then people began to eat bark and twigs. Realizing that doom was impending, a group of fifteen, dubbed *the Forlorn Hope*, set out in the snow-covered mountains to look for help. Soon they were lost and on the verge of starvation.

The fifteen men drew straws to see who would be eaten; however, malnutrition struck three of them before anyone had to be killed. The other members of the Forlorn Hope wrapped their dead companions in packages and carefully labeled them so nobody would be forced to eat a relative.

Six members of the Forlorn Hope eventually survived and stumbled onto a cabin to tell the terrible truth of what had happened. Rescue teams were dispatched to find the rest of the party. When the relief party finally stumbled on the rest of the Donner Party, they were witness to one of the worst single scenes in human history.

"Half-eaten bodies" lay strewn all over the place. One rescuer reported that the survivors "looked more like demons than human beings, surrounded by the remains of their unholy feast."

***

The PCT comes right over Donner's Pass, where this tragedy unfolded. Predictably, hikers (including this one) refer to it as 'Dahmer's Pass', named after the infamous modern day cannibal, Jeffrey Dahmer. All jokes aside, the comparison couldn't be more off the mark.

Jeffrey Dahmer's story is a morbid tale of human evil. On the other hand, if you really think about it, the party of George Donner mostly exhibited what we would refer to as positive human traits— pursuit of dreams, enormous energy, bravery, loyalty, and amazing survival instincts.

One of the Donner Party members had convinced everyone to try a shortcut, which ultimately failed and cost them several days. If not for that, the entire party would have arrived intact. But for somebody that has been lost as much as me, I'm uncomfortable even second-guessing that decision.

Yes, cannibalism is among the most gut-wrenching prospects a human could ever face, whichever side of the equation you happen to be on. But who can honestly say what they'd do in such a situation? It's a very sobering tale, indeed.

Chapter 30

Northern California Tales— Psychological Crucible

"Somebody could steal our backpacks," Fran said.

"Yeah, what else?" her fiancée, Double Barrel, asked skeptically.

"Maybe some injury that makes you get off the trail, but then heals quickly," Fran suggested. "A foot or something."

"Yeah, maybe," Double Barrel responded, still unexcited. "How about if somebody stole our credit card. People have to get off for things like that." This seemed to pick their attitude up, but it didn't help mine one bit.

Fran and Double Barrel had been a couple days behind me most of the way. Now they had caught up. You might think they had a head of steam. But, in fact, they were absolutely miserable with this heat and endless hiking. They desperately wanted off the trail, altogether. But they wouldn't allow themselves to do so. Why?

Like so many hikers, they had begun with great ceremony in their respective hometowns. Quitting—at least according to this logic— would be a humiliation. At least quitting for the sake of quitting. But if something strange happened to them so that they had to get off; well, that was another matter. Thus, this perverted conversation in Sierra City, that I sat there listening to with a kind of morbid fascination.

As you might expect, they weren't around much longer.

"SkyWalker," came a familiar voice from the top of the hill.

"*No Pain*," I exulted. "I don't believe it."

He was the first PCT hiker I had seen in three days. But he was going south.

"Where the hell are you going?" I asked.

"I hitched up to northern California and am hiking south to tell everybody goodbye?"

"You're getting off?"

"Northern California is endless, man. I want out."

This was a bit depressing. Here was a multiple-time AT hiker that appeared to have become totally disillusioned with the PCT. Worse yet, some of the non-AT hikers had been repeatedly pressing the theme: "The AT hikers don't do well on the PCT." I didn't have much ego as a hiker, but I didn't want people gaining pleasure that another AT alum had bought the dust.

No Pain was the only African-American on the trail, as far as I knew. Both the PCT and the AT cast very wide nets in terms of their hiking populations. But there is one great exception. Both trails are vastly underrepresented by members of the nation's two largest ethnic minorities—African-Americans and Hispanics. *Why?* My best guess is that it's a matter of basic geography. Neither African-Americans nor Latinos have ever settled heavily in mountainous regions. Honestly, it's a shame. Long-Distance hiking is a great unifier. Things like skin color and national origin fade completely into the background given the demanding day-in, day-out challenges that one faces. Which is why is was so disappointing to see No Pain quitting.

"You should see everybody—they all look like shit," No Pain said. "Dirk's all shriveled up. And everybody's depressed, too."

"Yeah, I'm just trying to hang in there, myself," I said. "But, God, it's impossible to stop the weight hemorrhaging."

"Man, you look really frail," he said staring at me.

We embraced and went our separate ways. From what I later heard from other hikers that he passed further south, No Pain used much more vivid adjectives than 'frail' to describe my physical appearance. He probably was right about that. But

I liked the struggle. It had great clarity to it, and I planned to see it through.

***

My best friend at this point may have been *Magic Man*. This was in spite of the fact that I hardly ever saw him. He was more like *Jack the Ripper*. He operated in the shadows, and you never knew when he was going to strike.

Magic Man's daughter, Boo-Boo (mentioned earlier) had tried to glissade down Sonora Pass, the last really snowy pass in the Sierras. Unfortunately, she was wearing shorts and picked up so many ice-shards in her legs that she was disabled for two weeks. Her father, Magic Man, had volunteered to come down from Washington State and help her make up for the lost time. In these remote, dry, and even lonely parts, he was constantly finding dirt roads in the middle of nowhere to leave water, Gatorade, and snacks. This was no ordinary water or Gatorade, either. Certain days it seemed like no matter how much water you drank, you still felt dehydrated.

One afternoon I approached a road, running very low on water. In fact, it was the second straight 'bad water day'. The previous afternoon I had wound down some steep mountain and been excited to hear the Feather River roaring at full-speed, its white capped currents shimmering in the brilliant mid-day sun. I had hurriedly picked my way down a large series of boulders in order to dip my water bottles and chug up. The problem is that the water in these wide, gorgeous rivers can double you over almost the minute you finish drinking it. At the campsite that night I repeatedly had to rush to relieve my diarrhea.

On this second day, morale had been even more fragile from the beginning. I had been thirsty all morning. The only water source listed in our data books was a creek that was over a mile off the trail, down a steep hill. I was dreading the thought of having to go down and retrieve it, and then having to hump all the way back up.

But when I had turned the corner before the road, there was the blue cooler. *Oh, man, oh, yeah, baby, yeah, yeah, be there baby, talk to me, talk to me,* I kept saying to myself as I drew closer.

I opened it. It was full of ice-cold liquids. *Oh sweet, Magic Man.* Uncharacteristically, I pumped my fist. It allowed me to hike until dark and get in my 25 miles for the day, as well as to get a good and well-hydrated start the next day.

Perhaps, the case of Magic Man was instructive. On the face of it, he had everything a person could ask for, including a good job, a nice family, and plenty of money. However, Thoreau's famous remark—"the great masses of people live in silent desperation,"—comes to mind.

Magic Man was taking his annual two-week summer vacation driving up dirt roads, shuttling around nauseous-smelling hikers, and filling up coolers. Juxtapose this against the normally plush, but sedentary, vacation he typically took. Without a doubt, he will remember this more plebeian vacation in the summer of '09 with much greater nostalgia. Trail life had caught his imagination.

***

"Thank you, honestly, we all appreciate it," I said to all the AmeriCorps volunteers, gathered on their hands and knees carving away at the trail. I was racing past them at maximum speed on the steep 4,500 foot descent into Belden. But the lower the trail descended, the more suffocating the heat became.

"You're doing great work," I kept saying. "Please just make sure you drink enough water."

"What's the hardest part of the trail? When did you start? How tall are you?" came back the questions in rapid-fire fashion. I wanted to chat, but this was dangerous heat. So I hurried down the mountain to get to Belden.

Meanwhile, I was faced with a steep 4,700 foot climb out of this steamy valley in gripping heat. By this point, I had begun measuring a climb as much in terms of calories expended as the actual difficulty of the mountain. The only antidote I knew of was to try and stuff myself with hamburgers, milkshakes, and French fries at the Belden General store. In four hours, I was able to get down almost 4,000 calories. Of course, that can sometimes be different from keeping them down.

I unenthusiastically walked out, bloated belly and all, and hoisted my backpack.

"Where are you going?" another hiker asked.

"Gonna' try to get this climb out of the way," I said.

"It's over a hundred," he said. "Wait."

"I wanna' get to Myrtle Flat Camp before dark," I said. So off I went, full of cheeseburger and milkshake. Too full. The results were predictable.

The trail followed steep ledges as it wound up the mountain. A steep embankment was on my right and a sharp dropoff was to the left. That left nowhere for an emergency bathroom run. It was painful. Most of all, it was frustrating. I probably lost all 4,000 calories within two miles of leaving Belden from fiery diarrhea explosions.

And I could just imagine my trailing colleagues coming up on this ghoulish scene, rolling their eyes, and muttering, "That poor fucking idiot, Skywalker."

Chapter 31

California Fires

"Hey Ralph," I yelled excitedly. "You goin' back up to the trail?"

"Yeah, get in," he said.

I ran across the street and threw my backpack in the back of his truck. It was always a relief to finally get a hitch, especially for us males.

"Did you hear about the fires?" Ralph asked.

"No."

"You had to hear all that lightning last night."

"Yeah, I was lying in my tent quaking half the night,"
I said.

"Well, it struck all along the trail just north of here."

"Is it safe to hike?" I asked.

"Not from what I'm hearing."

Like every American, I'm accustomed to watching television reports every summer of firemen doggedly battling out-of-control blazes in the West. However, since I had begun considering a PCT hike I had periodically worried about just what in the world hikers do in these situations. I was about to find out.

"Where's *Pepperoni*?" I asked. Ralph was the husband of Pepperoni (mentioned earlier as attempting to be the first woman to ever thru-ride the PCT).

"Headed right for the fires," he said, sounding concerned. "I don't know if she knows about them or not."

"How about if I hang with you?" I asked.

"Sure thing," he said. "I'm supposed to meet her tomorrow

at Hat Creek Rim. But the Forest Service tells me there may be some fires burning between here and there."

***

Other than the melting of the two polar ice-caps, the best evidence of global warming may be found in the staggering increase in western wildfires. Since 2000, more than 7,000,000 acres a year have been burned by wildland fires, which is more than double the rate of the previous four decades. The greatest increase has been at higher elevations because of earlier snowmelt.

Yet the increase in average temperature has been just one degree Fahrenheit. That is especially troubling for the simple reason that there are projections for even greater temperature increases in the future. In fact, burning wildfires may soon become one of the central facts of life in the West. To be sure, with my lack of scientific background, I'm a pretty easy lay when I read these articles and statistics. But now I was seeing it with my own eyes.

And I'd never seen anything quite like it. On the highway down to Old Station, black halos rose from various locations towards the sky. The firefighters had one highway blocked off and the town of Old Station was shut down.

Ralph and I camped along a dirt road, and got up early to try to find Pepperoni. When we got to the Hat Creek Rim parking lot, tourists were gathered around the overlook checking out the valley below, which was smothered by dark fumes. This was the same valley Pepperoni needed to ride through to get here.

"Ralph, there's no way she's gonna' go through that," I said.

"You don't know my wife," he shot back.

"I know she's determined," I said, "but she's not crazy."

"I'm telling you," he said red-faced. "you don't know my wife. She will not quit."

For the next forty-five minutes we debated, increasingly intensely, whether his wife would try to ascend up to Hat Creek Rim. As the smoke became denser and people started to scurry off in their cars, I began wondering just how smart it was for the two of us to be hanging out here, ourselves.

"Ralph, let's go check out the hiker hostel down in Old Station," I suggested. "Somebody's probably seen Pepperoni."

"I told her I'd meet her here," he said tensely.

"She's not coming up here," a bystander piped in.

"I'm telling the two of ya," he raged. "You don't know my wife."

Finally, as the smoke became a black pall, he relented and pulled the horse truck out onto the road to head down into the valley. *I'd better be right about this.*

"Hey, there's Miles," I said excitedly. "Let's see if he knows anything."

"Have you seen my wife?" Ralph asked.

"Yeah, we were together all morning, but she wanted to ride to the next road."

"See," Ralph said, "she never quits."

"Well," I said relieved. "we should be able to find her."

"Mind if I get in?" Miles asked.

"Yeah, load your pack up," Ralph said. *Great.* Miles was about my age and the perfect trail gentleman. He'd be a good guy to hang out with the next few days as I tried to figure out how to navigate theses fires.

Ralph parked the van off to the side of the highway and we headed out in three directions searching for his wife. Just in the last fifteen minutes a new halo of black smoke was coming from what looked like no more than a few hundred yards to the north of where we were. Finally, Pepperoni appeared nobly on her horse.

"Did you see that fire burning just up the trail?" she said amazed.

"Yes," the three of us said in unison. Ralph and she hugged. I went over to begin throwing out suggestions for what we should all do next.

"Hey Skywalker," Miles wisely whispered, "Come here for a second. Just give 'em a little time together."

Ralph and Pepperoni quickly decided on a plan they had long considered. They were going to drive to Canada so that Pepperoni could begin riding south on the PCT. That would lengthen her riding season.

"Aren't you going to miss everybody?" I asked Pepperoni. "You're going to be alone all the time."

"Yeah, but I don't have any choice. I need more time."

Pepperoni had really gotten her sea legs the last few hundred miles. She was maneuvering her horses much better through the mountain ranges. Most importantly, every fiber of her being was wrapped up in her attempt to thru-ride the PCT.

This inimitable twosome had defied the odds so far. But now, the two of them—along with their two horses—were heading off on a journey that would be of *great import*.

***

It was surreal—almost like a sick joke. I honestly couldn't believe my eyes.

"Man, this is worse than Old Station," I lamented to Miles. "We've gotta' get the hell out of here."

Miles and I had followed the suggestion of the Forest Service and caught the bus to Burney, California. But the closer we got to Burney, the smokier it was getting – almost like being in a steam room inundated with smoke. *Where is it coming from?*

But when we entered Burney Falls Park, we came upon a lady who had picked up a reputation as a hiker-friendly ranger.

"Is it okay to hike in this?" I immediately blurted out.

"Other hikers have gone out into it," she said.

"Today?"

"Yeah, this morning."

"But the park looks abandoned?" I noted.

"Yeah," she said. "But some of the PCT hikers hiked out."

That was not the answer I wanted to hear. Nonetheless, I reluctantly set off north on the smoke-filled PCT. *This is the strangest thing I've ever done.*

I reckon a lot of hikers would make good poker players. By its very nature, long-distance hiking carried certain existential risks—snakes, bears, hypothermia, getting lost, serious injury— that your average person didn't confront regularly. A stiff upper lip was almost a like an unwritten code. I was trying to get there myself, but had quite a ways to go. And hiking with forest fires raging in the vicinity was a new danger that I simply wasn't mentally prepared for.

After two miles, Miles and I—along with a third hiker, Miner—arrived at Britton's dam, where scores of dam workers were hard at work. An especially black halo of smoke flared up somewhere over the top of the hill we were fixing to ascend.

"Excuse me, sir," I rushed up to a group of the dam workers. "Do you think it's safe for us to hike north from here?"

"You see this ravine here," one of them pointed further downstream. "A 1300 degree fire just jumped the banks. It was down in the water one minute and all the way at the top of that hill up there fifteen minutes later."

"How did you get it out?" I wondered.

"That's what we're doing here—releasing the bladder of the dam to drown it out."

"So I take it you don't reckon it's a good idea for us to continue?" I said, speaking loudly so that Miles and Miner could digest this. Several of the dam workers shook their head. The three of us stood there on the dam looking up at the hill where the PCT went. There was smoke (and obviously a fire) on the other side of this hill. But how far over the hill, we didn't know.

"I'm for turning back," I finally said. Perhaps that was predictable. I wasn't going to win the Intrepid Hiker Award. But this wasn't a junior-high spend-the-night party, either.

"Think about it," I reasoned. "We walk up there and the fire quickly spreads and engulfs us. Probably isn't gonna' happen, but it could. Okay. What happens then? In my case, my mother would investigate what happened and surely it comes out that a bunch of dam workers had explicitly warned us not to walk towards the fire. And what did we do? Walked straight into the inferno. So now my mother has to live with the fact that she raised not only a fool, but also a hopeless idiot."

"Yeah, I hear you," Miles said. "I don't want to go down in history as the guy who walked straight into a fiery death."

"But how do we know that fire isn't two miles over that hill?" Miner dissented in game fashion. Some hikers had been put off along the way by Miner's tics and quirks. But the more I had gotten to know him, the more I had started to like him. He was as authentic as the day is long.

"You're absolutely right," I said. "We don't know. But I'm not for finding out, either." I started backwards. Of course, a leadership role in the woods is rare for me, and this was a dubious one. But the other two slowly followed, although Miner kept looking back seemingly in a state of existential angst.

All the hotels in Burney were booked from firefighters coming in from all over the state; so we commenced looking for anywhere to stealth camp behind an office building or wherever.

"Any luck?" I asked when we ran into one of the firefighters in town.

His face said it all—utterly down in the mouth. "Wow," he finally admittedly. "it's got us on our heels pretty good."

Chapter 32

The Art of the Possible

Things happened fast.

"Some people talk about doing things like the PCT," the driver announced over the bus intercom. "Others do it." The other passengers looked at us like we were Roman gladiators as we piled out of the bus in the pouring rain. What our adoring audience didn't know was that one of was 'mudpieing' at this latest turn of events.

We had been planning to catch the bus 80 miles up the PCT to Castella. There we would re-supply to get back on the hopefully fire-free PCT, tomorrow. But the bus driver had other ideas. When he had seen us with our backpacks back at the station, he had immediately begun sermonizing on his long-lost ambition to hike the PCT, himself.

"I'll drop you off under the interstate right by the PCT," he volunteered.

"Yeah, that would be great," Miles said. Great, that is, if you have enough food. But the thing that worried me even more was it began to pour rain hard for the first time since we had begun the PCT. The firefighters had gotten a break. But had we?

Underneath the interstate bridge, I pulled out my wallet and convinced Miner to sell me some food. Then we took off on a hundred mile stretch with nary a town in between. Immediately, the specter of hypothermia appeared on my radar screen, as we climbed 4,000 feet up an exposed mountain. Taking care of one's extremities is extremely important in these situations. That's

In northern California with Miles, who got my nomination for the PCT True Gentleman Award. Why is he only wearing one glove?

why my mind was on the Lake Tahoe Post Office, which was 400 miles back. I had sat there with a package open, agonizing over whether to send my gloves forward to Ashland, Oregon. Finally, I had reasoned that it was blazing hot and I needed to get my backpack weight down. So I had put them in and saved myself two ounces.

"What an idiot I was," I said to Miles, "sending my gloves forward in Lake Tahoe." *Hint, hint.*

"You can have my mittens," he offered.

Problem solved. At least, solved for a few miles. The trail continued winding up to even colder, more exposed areas. By now, I had on several layers. And Miles' mittens.

"Any way we could share those mittens you're wearing?" Miles asked me self-consciously.

"Are you kidding?" I said embarrassed. "Take 'em. Thanks."

"No, no," he said, "we'll share them."

It would have been nice to have absolutely insisted that he take both his mittens back. But I needed it and rotated the mitten from one hand to the other for the next couple hours.

***

"Hey, Skywalker," a girl yelled down the hill.

"Hey," I said squinting my eyes at the girl crawling out of her tent. "Oh, *Poet*. What are you doing camped up there?"

"I couldn't quit shaking along this ridge yesterday," she said plainly.

"You alright?" I asked.

"Yeah," she said. "I definitely think I was at least a little hypothermic."

"Come hike with us," I suggested.

"That would be great."

It was good timing.

"I was 95% sure I was quitting when I got to town," she said. "I've been alone practically the whole time the last 500 miles." As it was, she and Miles hit it off immediately, and were destined to hike together the remaining 1,200 miles.

Poet was in her late twenties and lived in Dutch Harbor, Alaska, where she worked for the Fishing and Game Service. The temperature never exceeded the mid-fifties on this outer island, but she was sturdily built. I had wondered if she was gay, and she quickly removed that mystery in one of our free-flowing conversations.

"I'm not a Christian anymore," she said, "because they're the reason I can't marry my girlfriend." Actually though, from what I've seen, hiking trails are pretty good places for gays in general. Narrow-minded bigots are an endangered species out here.

***

You never saw such a mismatch. On the one hand, you had a couple dozen members of a historical society. They had car loads full of food and beer, and were well-rested and clean. On the other hand, there was a group of famished, dirty hikers that hadn't seen town in several days. Who had the advantage? The hikers by a long-shot.

Miles, Poet, and I had hiked our 25 miles and arrived at the Scott Mountain campsite just before dark. This group of Shriners had camp all set up as they tossed back beers. Barbecued chicken, corn and potatoes were being cooked. We didn't say anything to each other. Everybody instinctively knew what to do. Develop camaraderie. Quickly.

"Would ya'll like beers?" one fellow soon asked us.

"Oh gee, if you've got an extra."

"Sure, we've got plenty."

They riddled us with one question after another, and our answers sounded like they came out of a travel brochure. I was reminded of how a wolf attacks a pigpen. They come up and begin licking the pig's ear warmly to draw it out of the pen. At that point the wolf goes for the kill. We weren't quite as ruthless.

But soon one of the more inebriated members mouthed off, "You know, we brought lots of chicken. We might have some extra."

"Golly," I said as if it had come as a surprise, "that would be incredible, but please don't feel obligated."

I had one concern, though. It was a selfish one and completely out of the spirit of the PCT. We had passed a foursome called the *Dog Pack* that morning. Their names were Five Dollar, Strider, Oz, and Waffles. They often slept cowboy style in the middle of the trail. This morning, we had stepped over and around them to get past. This young foursome had become legendary for a couple different things: hiking very long distances at a time and chasing women in trail towns like there was no tomorrow. They were erratic, and you never knew quite where they were going to show up.

Right as the Shriners were counting out the number of hikers and pieces of chicken, the Dog Pack showed up. They sidled up to me and Five Dollar whispered excitedly, "Hey Skywalker, who are these guys?"

"They're handing out beers," I let on.

"Yeah cool," Waffles said. "Are they gonna' feed people?"

Ultimately, my sense of obligation won out over my craving for the food.

"It's looking like we've got a beachhead," I said choosing my words carefully. "But we're not feeling completely secure yet."

I began introducing them and trying to integrate them in with the Shriners. Fortunately, these folks found a way to feed all of us, with second helpings and desserts included. Then, the toastmaster announced, "Let's have some campsite humor."

Immediately, a man to my left who looked to be pushing 80, asked, "What's the difference between a peeping-tom and a pickpocket?"

No answer. "A pickpocket snatches watches," he announced logically.

Not bad. My turn.

I couldn't control myself at joke time any better than at food time.

"They took a poll of how many women smoked after sex," I announced. "Ninety-nine percent of women said they did not know, because they never had looked."

More racy humor followed (I even felt the need to make an awkward apology to Poet the next day). You could feel the Shriners becoming weary, and probably wondering if they had made a good food investment. We hikers silently filed away—with full stomachs to be sure—to pitch our tents.

In the morning, though, we noticed they had brought out mountains of bacon and eggs. Again, we all went into action. Individually, everybody walked up to where they were cooking the food, all with the express purpose of thanking them for the previous night. Of course, we had ulterior motives.

"Can't thank you enough," I ritually said on my passage up. "We'll be bragging about this to all our colleagues on the trail." But they all held firm and bid us crisp, "happy hiking" farewells.

Back on the trail after about five miles, we all took a break together at a water source. Everybody unenthusiastically pulled out our pop tarts, crackers, and peanut butter, and went about their business.

"Wonder why they didn't offer us any more food this morning?" Five Dollar asked.

"It looked like they just kinda' decided we were all fucked," Waffles opined.

"Yeah." Everybody shook their head matter-of-factly. Nobody

spoke of it again. Just trail business.

Fortunately, we had the powerful white-capped eminence of Mount Shasta at 14,179 feet to console us today. "When I first caught sight of it," John Muir memorably said, "my blood turned to wine, and I haven't been weary ever since."

***

At twilight everybody got stuck out on another narrow saddle for several miles. There was nowhere to camp, which seemed like a theme playing out more and more in surprisingly rugged northern California.

Poet and I were in the vanguard and kept throwing out ideas as the last daylight dimmed.

"What about there?" she would ask.

"Too steep to sleep."

"I just don't see anything flatter," she correctly observed.

"My map shows a dirt road coming up somewhere here," I said. "There is usually somewhere to camp near those."

Finally, I dropped my backpack and ran off to do some reconnaisance. Soon, I found the dirt road. But it had a steep shoulder on one side and a dropoff on the other.

"Hey, why don't we put our tents up on the road," I suggested. "That's the only flat spot."

"Yeah," she said unenthusiastically, "but look here—see the fresh tire marks." There was absolutely nowhere else to camp. However, I did see some downed trees.

"Hey Poet," I suggested, "how about helping me haul some of these trees out here. We can lay them across the road about 50 yards above and below us. A car would crash into the trees before us." She was skeptical at first, but soon we had our sleeping territory in the middle of the road cordoned off from any vehicle traffic. The other hikers liked it as well, and about ten of us camped right in the middle of the road. In fact, it was a technique I would end up using several times further up the trail when I couldn't find anywhere to camp as dark approached.

Heck, even I could be a little creative out here when necessity demanded it.

Chapter 33

California Leavin'

It was undoubtedly the worst seven miles of the PCT—paved road walk—to possibly the worst trail town on the PCT. But I was desperate to get there.

For starters, hiking on steaming asphalt with the sun beating down on you is simply no fun. But more importantly, was the great hiker obsession—food. There was a restaurant in Seiad Valley that closed on Sunday afternoons. But I didn't know what time. It was a classic tradeoff. The faster I went, the more calories I would burn; but the better chance I had of eating some real food. So I walked at maximum speed.

A southbounder appeared in the distance. I hadn't seen another hiker in days (after finally crying uncle in my strenuous attempt to keep up with Miles and Poet), and normally would

Trailside breaks are a hiker's best friend.

have been quite chatty. But today, I was all business.

"Excuse me, do you know what time the restaurant closes in Seiad Valley?"

"I think 2:30," he said.

"Do you have the time?"

"2:00." "Thanks." A half-hour later a truck came up from behind me.

"Would you like a ride, sir?" the driver asked with a knowing smile.

Without hesitation, I threw my backpack and myself in the back of his truck for the last three miles. When we neared what looked like the restaurant in this two-building town, he yelled back, "Usually hikers have me drop 'em off a couple hundred yards in front of the store, so nobody can see they got a ride. Do you want me to do that?"

"No thanks," I said. "To the store please." I practically burst into the air-conditioned restaurant where a few hikers were finishing up their lunch.

"Are you still serving?" I asked the lady behind the counter.

"Just finished up," she said.

I looked deeply into her eyes, somehow trying to show a passion—or craving—for food theretofore unknown to her.

"Would it help if I beg?" I finally asked. Unlike the Shriners, this woman had seen her share of hikers. She wasn't outmatched. "No it wouldn't," she answered me crisply. "We're through today."

***

There were only 35 miles left in California, but that included a 5,400 foot ascent. At least calories weren't a problem, though. Tradition requires hikers to try the *five-pound pancake challenge* in Seiad Valley. That's a tall order in any event. And it was made more difficult by something I had kept hearing on the trail.

"I hear they're not very good." They weren't. A strapping hiker from New Zealand named *Heaps* had knocked out 3½ pounds, but nobody else even came close. My effort was abysmal.

I was wobbly from pancake mix as I wandered down the road

out of Seiad Valley in 100 degree-plus weather. My backpack was running about 45 pounds from carrying five liters of water. Some hikers had hauled alcoholic spirits out of Seiad Valley to celebrate the border crossing. Not me. To be sure, it was a pretty big deal. After all, I'd been in California 3 ½ months, which was at least two weeks longer than I had anticipated.

Within a mile of the border, the trail was running high along a ridge overlooking Donomore Creek. Suddenly, I heard a ruckus of heavy crashing and thrashing on the steep hill that lay between me and the creek. There was only one possible explanation. *Where is it? More importantly, which way is it running?*

Fortunately, I heard more thunderous steps and commotion further down the hill. Finally, a medium-sized brown bear tumbled out of the woods into Donomore Creek. Many times in the day while hiking (but never at night!) I had fantasized about what the perfect bear encounter would look like. This was it. I was no longer scared to death of bears on a daily basis, which I guess is an accomplishment of sorts. But to see one is to respect their awesome power.

Unfortunately, the older couple I had camped with the previous evening had been planning to camp here at Donamore Creek. I left them a note on the trail alerting them to the presence of a bear in the neighborhood. They later told me it convinced them to hike on.

I then crossed the well-signed border, but could find nowhere better to camp than alongside a fairly prominent dirt road with ravines dropping off on both sides. This time it was a much smaller animal I heard tiptoeing around my tent in the dark—*cougar, coyote, raccoon?* At first I though I was imagining it, because the steps were so light.

"Who's that? Who's that?" I kept calling out.

Silence. Then I would hear the unmistakable steps of a four-legged animal. I had company. This animal probably traveled this road every night, but had never seen a tent alongside it.

I was now in Oregon. But I had been in California so long my mind still lay there. All my life, I had gotten bent out of shape listening to Californians describing their state as the be-all, end all—a veritable earthly utopia. Now, however, after traveling the length of the state I could at least see where these people were coming from.

"Everything starts in California," is the state's reputation. Objectively, they have lived up to their billing. In the 1960's, the antiwar protests and sexual revolution received their greatest impetus here. In the 1970's, California Governor Ronald Reagan spearheaded the nationwide revolt against higher taxes. In the 1990's, California became the first state to outlaw smoking in all public places, a trend that was soon replicated across the country. What's next?

PCT hikers had been amazed back in the desert when we passed through thousands and thousands of wind turbines. "Hey, at least we're trying something," several people had remarked. Also, I had at first been confused in trail towns coming upon so many unflushed toilets (various signs overhanging the toilet recommended one flush every four urinations). My attempt to replicate this back home at my mother's house was met with great ridicule from my mother! In any event, hiking the PCT fits right in with California's next great revolution—energy independence. After all, who has a lower carbon footprint than a long-distance hiker?

I had had a 'California deficit' when I arrived in the state to hike the PCT, having spent a mere three days in my life in the Golden State. I had learned on the Appalachian Trail that the best way to erase a geographical deficit on your resume is to cover the place on foot.

Now it was time to erase my geographical deficits in Oregon and Washington – neither of which I'd ever been to. There would be a great opportunity to do so, as 1,000 miles of traveling by foot lay ahead of me. Like all hikers, I greatly looked forward to it. The big question was whether I had enough time.

Chapter 34

An Eastern Man of the West

*No man can really understand our country
unless he has the fullest and closest sympathy
with the ideals and aspirations of the West.*

Theodore Roosevelt

"Go West, young man. Go West!"

Such was the spirit of the age in the latter half of the 19th century. Some of the most unlikely young men took this sentiment to heart.

One of them was a sickly little boy from an aristocratic family in New York City. His name was Theodore Roosevelt. Young Teddy chafed at the restrictions of city life. He even attempted to self-educate himself about zoology on the streets of Manhattan, and resolved to learn the songs of every bird in Central Park. In middle-American terms, he could easily have been called a *nerd*.

Roosevelt's father spent a small fortune taking his family all over Europe to meet royalty and see the great cathedrals, castles, and museum. These were privileges most people could only dream of. But young Theodore became bored by it all. He wanted to prove his manhood. Deep down he thought his best chance to do this was in the West.

What followed was a lifelong affair with the entire region.

***

The more one studies Theodore Roosevelt, it becomes apparent that more than perhaps any other person, he embodies the American character, in both its strengths and weaknesses.

For many people, both inside and outside the United States, the westward expansion is the most compelling part of the entire American epic. Behind it all lay *Manifest Destiny*—the idea that God willed that all the land between the Atlantic and Pacific Oceans belong to the United States. No one was a greater believer in this than Theodore Roosevelt. Roosevelt loved war, and actually thought the United States had not seized enough land in the Mexican-American War of 18461848. He even believed that parts that of the Canadian provinces were rightfully American.

Roosevelt was a staunch advocate of the so-called *strenuous life,* and its cult of action, rough individualism, and adventurous romance. He worried greatly that with the frontier coming to an end, the American male would lose his virility. In its place would follow an "*overcivilized* man who has lost the great fighting virtues."

Roosevelt's first trip to the West in 1883 occurred amid a backdrop of stunning devastation. The buffalo population had dwindled from 40,000,000 in 1800 to just 2,000 by 1883. The population of white tailed deer was similarly decimated, falling from 24,000,000 to 500,000. Nonetheless, Roosevelt gained a great sense of triumph by hunting and killing both.

***

When Roosevelt became President in 1901 upon McKinley's assassination, a few giant corporations (Standard Oil, railroad magnates) controlled huge chunks of the national economy. Worse yet, the nation's wilderness was under unrelenting assault—woodlands being heavily logged, wetlands being drained, streams being fished out—especially in the West. The new western-loving president immediately decided to sharply change course.

"A people without children would face a hopeless future," he said. "A country without trees is almost as hopeless."

To Roosevelt the West—particularly the dry mountain air of the Rockies and the warm climate of California and the Southwest—was a cure for America's industrial ills. He even predicted that someday the population of the West would equal that of the east of the Mississippi River (a stunning, but eventually true prediction).

The federal government had to play the key role. Roosevelt decided it should take over ownership and management of public lands. His U.S. Forest Service director, the famed Gifford Pinchot, became the most powerful member of his cabinet.

"The only time I ever see the President," his Secretary of State Elihu Root lamented, "is when he comes rushing past me to get to Pinchot."

In Douglass Brinkley's magnificent groundbreaking biography of Roosevelt, *Wilderness Warrior*, Brinkley colorfully shows how Roosevelt and Pinchot warred with all manner of special interests on behalf of wilderness.

"Gifford Pinchot, the U.S. Forester, has done more to retard the growth and development of the Northwest than any other man," fumed the Governor of Washington.

In 1907 Congress, finally was on the verge of folding from the pressure of irate corporations and land developers. Just minutes before the congressional session began, however, Roosevelt signed an executive order setting aside 16,000,000 acres for the U.S. Forest Service.

"The opponents of the Forest Service turned handsprings in their wrath," Roosevelt chortled. Timber companies immediately sued and two cases went to the Supreme Court. The Court decided in Roosevelt's favor in both cases.

Roosevelt and Pinchot ultimately quadrupled the nation's forest reserves. Altogether, 234 million acres of American wilderness were saved. Five national parks, including the scenically wondrous Crater Lake and Grand Canyon National Parks were established during the Roosevelt administration. For that reason, some have rhetorically referred to him as our first western President. His motivation was at least partly a competitive attitude towards our European rivals. In Roosevelt's mind, our natural wonders offered greater national prestige than such European citadels of culture as the Louvre or Westminister Abbey.

Historians have traditionally awarded its highest echelons to winners of wars (Washington, Lincoln, Franklin Roosevelt) and practicioners of power politics (Jefferson, Reagan). For that reason, history probably hasn't caught up yet with the drastic, long-lasting changes that Theodore Roosevelt's administration wrought right here at home in our nation's very geography.

From a personal standpoint, I probably would not have the opportunity, along with many other Americans, to attempt a linear thru-hike through such breathtaking scenery all the way from Mexico to Canada, without the decisive actions taken a century ago by this eastern patrician, who so fell in love with the West.

Chapter 35

Uber Bitch

Just remember this. Anybody's personal quota of height-related question is three. So when the waitress at the lunch counter in Ashland, Oregon had violated that by at least double, I had a bit of an attitude. Then she asked me about bears.

"The only thing you really need to know," I spouted out "is that 83% of hikers are males, but 83% of hikers that get eaten by bears are females."

"Where do you get this bologna from?" a voice from behind me had immediately asked. I turned around and looked into the sunburned, freckly face of a dark-haired, middle-aged woman of indeterminate ethnic origin. The Long Island accent was unmistakable. So was her I-don't-suffer-fools gladly attitude.

After a bit of towel-snapping style back and forth between us, she introduced herself.

"I'm *Uber Bitch* by the way," she said. I noticed she looked directly into my eye when she made the introduction. Undoubtedly, she got some enjoyment out of studying the reactions of her fellow hikers upon making this introduction. My grade was probably about average.

I waited a couple minutes before non-chalantly asking, "So, did you pick up your trail name at the Kickoff?"

"No," she replied matter-of-factly. "My *husband* gave it to me."

***

I didn't have many complaints about the PCT. My biggest one was a bit counter-intuitive, in fact. There just weren't enough crappy hikers out here. Actually, there weren't any of these left at all. The PCT is no more difficult than the Appalachian Trail. But, it is more intimidating. Many had met their fate in the broiling desert. It's too bad. Like bad students, bad employees, bad golfers, bad you-name-it, bad hikers are often the ones with the best senses of humor. A bigger concern than the lack of cripples, was that there weren't enough average hikers out here.

I kept running into this group—the famously libidinous, Dog Pack. There was nothing average about them, whether it be their hiking mileage, drinking and eating habits, sexual prowess (or so they claimed!), or hiking schedules. Actually, I saw them every day— sometimes several times. When they were actually hiking I couldn't keep up with them. But they were prone to several hours of breaks per day, followed by night-hiking that often left them sprawled out on the middle of the trail where I would step over them the next morning. It worked for them, and they sure were colorful. But it never would have worked for me.

At the big hiker hostel in the famous counter-culture mecca of Ashland, Das Boots cooked a fabulous meal for everyone. Miraculously, it was also healthy and, unlike hiker food which is almost all brown, all colors were represented. Das Boots showed his good humor by wearing a yellow-blazer, fessing up to the fact that he had hitchhiked (on the yellow blaze of the highway) most of northern California. Then he announced he was quitting right there in Ashland.

I got to chatting with Uber Bitch again. She even dropped her 'fess-up wiseguy' attitude and leveled a bit with me.

"I was hiking with my husband and stepdaughter every step of the way the first 1,600 miles," she said. "But they both had to get off."

"Bummer," I said.

"Yeah, well he's 70 years old, and kills himself out here," she said.

"Who've you been hiking with since?" I asked.

"Nobody," she quickly said. "Absolutely nobody. And I swear

to God, within 200 yards of saying goodbye to my husband and leaving Seiad Valley, what happens? I run into a bear. It wasn't that big of a deal, but you know how it is. When you camp alone, the phobias start to set in."

"Well, I know all the Dog Pack will find an excuse to stay in town another day," I said. "But I'm headed out in the morning. You're welcome to join me."

"Alright," she said.

"How many miles a day do you hike?" I asked. In this case, it was not an egocentric question—just logical.

"Twenty-five," she stoutly said. She was fifty years old and barely over five-feet tall. I was almost 49, 6'11", and sported a wasting away frame.

"Yeah," I replied, "that's what I'm trying for too."

This conversation was to prove momentous for both of us. She later told me just how close she had come to throwing in the towel in right here in Ashland. And given that it was now August, and an early Canadian winter loomed, she would turn out to be just the right influence for me.

***

If the sedentary lifestyle is your cup of tea, the Duck State is just not the kind of place you'd choose. The state's outdoor culture is vibrant. Eugene, Oregon, in fact, may be the physical fitness capital of the world. Hood River on the other side of the state revolves almost entirely around water sports. And Oregonians like to hike. I liked that. By my lights, we got plenty of solitude in this continent-long quest, and it was good to see some fresh new faces.

The mountain range is the Cascades. Most of these mountains are, in fact, volcanoes. Often you find yourself walking on the flotsam and jetsam of volcanoes that exploded millions of years back, and it has created a relatively level landscape. This was a PCT hiker's chance to make up for lost time, or at least that's what we'd been telling ourselves all the way through California.

"I think it's right up here," I pointed to the driver chauffeuring us back up to the trailhead.

"No, no, don't listen to a word he says," Uber Bitch jumped in with her saucy style. "Just keep going."

Oh boy, what's this gonna' be like.

Uber Bitch and I set out together and hiked until dark. Again, the only place we could find to camp was a dirt road. You've got givers and takers in this world. Fortunately, it quickly became apparent she was the former.

"Here go, that spot looks best for your long tent," she said, offering me the only flat spot on the dirt road. I then introduced Uber Bitch to the routine of hauling logs out to cordon off the road, and she gamely took to that.

"I'll be off by 6:30," she told me before getting into our tents.

A lot of hikers say this at night (including, occasionally me), but 49% or less actually do it. Uber Bitch consistently did it. She wasn't fast. She made up for it by an early starting time, cutting her breaks shorter than everybody else's, and hiking until almost dark. It was an impressive effort to watch.

In her favor, she did have some considerable outdoor experience to call on. Just a couple years back, she and her husband had ridden their bicycles around the world. She was also quite adept in map reading, and more than just in the conventional sense of not getting lost. There were long waterless stretches on the PCT in Oregon. But there were also many different trails to accommodate the denizens of this outdoor-mad state.

"Hey," she would point out. "We could take.." Next thing you know we'd be following some trail that often looked as much like a rabbit trail, as a hiking trail.

"Are you sure this is right?' I would ask.

"Yes, look," and she would show me the route.

Very few of us were virgins at this point, and some of the PCT guidebooks even recommended these side trails as more scenic and less waterless than the PCT. Often these routes wound along lakes, which had me skittish. They were our water sources. But then I ran into a hydrologist on the trail.

"I was a hydrologist for the state of California for thirty-six years," he said. "I can assure you that lake water is a better bet than water out of any stream."

"Gosh, I had always just assumed running water was better," I said.

"No, all the animal excrement in the lake sinks to the bottom," he answered. "but it can float along the top of running water.

"Just make sure you filter it," he added.

Soon I became comfortable enough drinking out of these lakes.

***

"Who is that?' I yelled out of my tent.

It had to be at least 3:00 a.m. in the morning. My tent was lying about a foot off the PCT (Uber Bitch was a few yards back) right where we had wound up at dark the previous evening.

"Is that you Backtrack?" I questioned the person.

"Yeah," Backtrack answered. "Who is that? Skywalker?"

"Yeah."

I heard others with him.

"What the hell are ya'll doing?" I asked.

"Fifty-eight miles," came another familiar-sounding voice.

It was Hollywood, and I also heard Pink's familiar cadences in the background. Pink and Hollywood had met early on in the desert, and hit it off immediately. For a basic reason. They both fit the right profile.

Hollywood was in his late twenties, had studied acting in university, and aspired to greatness. To be honest, I didn't quite understand why it had eluded him so far, given his matinee-idol looks and dry wit. Pink (always wore pink colors) sure hadn't eluded him. She was in her early twenties and may have been the sexiest thing that ever walked on two legs. She practically worshipped the ground Hollywood walked on. Good for them. But, as was so often the case with trail romances, not so good for a couple folks back home.

"I saw her making out with a different guy," Uber Bitch had told me one day, after Pink and Hollywood walked by.

"Must have been before she met Hollywood," I said, confused.

"No," she said firmly. "Just recently. *He* was sitting right there watching."

Then someone had revealed the truth to us. This third person was Pink's boyfriend back home. Hollywood had employed the same subterfuge. A couple weeks after Pink's boyfriend had visited, Hollywood's long-time girlfriend from San Francisco had arrived for a few days of hiking with her long-time mate. Pink, of course, became the supernumerary this time. On both occasions, Hollywood and Pink had introduced the other to their respective lovers, as a mere hiking partner.

Not shocking news, of course, that this would all happen. The PCT is like Las Vegas, except more so. What happens out here, stays out here.

"What time is it?" I asked Backtrack, Hollywood, and Pink, as I lay there in my tent.

"4:00," Backtrack asked.

As I lay there groggily trying to hold up my end of the conversation, one thing was more than obvious. All three of their voices were soaked with adrenalin. Hollywood and Pink's previous longest day was 24 miles. They had started hiking about 21 hours ago, and wouldn't be finished for another 7 or hours; so technically, it wouldn't be a 58 mile day.

It was one heckuva' effort, to be sure. But big mile days were the great talisman. For starters, hikers couldn't resist bragging about them. Worse though, it took days to recover from the adrenaline hangover. The day-to-day grind became more of an uphill battle. Unfortunately, two of these three would become virtually disabled by this 58 mile Herculean effort. They would never be the same again.

***

I'm not an aesthete. To me there are very few places in the world that are worth traveling to for the sole purpose of seeing a sight. I'm a firm believer that it's the people you meet that make a trip.

However, there is no denying that there are a few places on this earth that command overwhelming awe at first sight (Grand Canyon, Yosemite). Until 7,000 years ago, Crater Lake was no such wonder. It didn't even exist. Rather, Mount Mazama was one of the volcanoes on the arc of the Cascade Range. But suddenly, around 5700 BCE, there was a massive volcanic explosion that transformed the landscape forever. After millions of years, Mount Mazama was suddenly no more. In its place was a massive crater that measured six miles wide. Given that the area gets an average of *533 inches of precipitation per year*, it quickly filled up and became known, appropriately, as Crater Lake. At 1,949 feet, it is the deepest lake in the United States, and bigger than all but Lake Tahoe and the Great Lakes.

The initial view is magical—not because of the size, but, rather, the intense blue color. Because most of the massive precipitation it receives is from snowfall, it is one of the clearest lakes in the world, with clarity readings of 120 feet. A twenty-mile circular ring of cliffs, crowned with Douglas firs and hemlocks, provides a stunning backdrop.

A big group of PCT hikers stopped at the very tastefully done *Rim Lodge*, a Depression Era CCC construction. Soon, everybody had stretched their tight hiker budgets to enjoy shrimp and beer while gazing out at this national wonder. It was as idyllic a moment as I've ever experienced. Everything was perfect. At least, it was until OSG's (Orange Shirt Guy's) cell-phone rang. A grave look soon came across OSG's face.

"Guys, you're not gonna believe what I just heard," he said, and then proceeded to relate a heart-rending tale.

Pepperoni and Ralph, of course, had left the bubble of northbound thru-hikers after the chaos of the forest fires, and driven to the Canadian border where she was going to ride south. Unfortunately, a major bridge-crossing was down in northern Washington. In the especially desolate stretches Pepperoni always had two horses—one to ride, and one to carry supplies— tied together by rope. When she had arrived at a ledge with an especially steep falloff, she had jumped off her riding horse and carefully led both horses with the rope.

Unfortunately, she had stumbled over some jagged terrain and went down hard on her face.

"It was just one of those things," she later recalled. "One minute I was walking along. Next thing you know, I'm on my face."

"You're lucky the horses didn't trample you?" I suggested.

"They saved my life *once again*," she quickly replied. "They jumped over me, but that sent them down the ravine."

"How long did you hold onto the rope after you fell?" I then asked her.

"Only a second, it was impossible."

But that one second was enough to send her 75 feet down the ravine. As she lay there woozy, she heard her horses crashing further down the hill.

Not only were her horses' lives on the line, but so was hers. All her food, water, and camping equipment were on the horses.

"I knew what had probably happened," she said with great emotion, "when I started seeing things strewn along the hill."

The two horses she had raised from birth were dead (They would soon be devoured by grizzly bears). Moreover, she was stranded in one of the most isolated areas in the United States. The thing that may have saved her was the controversial SPOT button. She hit it and several hours later an emergency rescue team arrived to evacuate her.

A noticeable pall fell over everybody gathered on the terrace at Crater Lake Lodge. Pepperoni's attempt at a thru-ride had earned our admiration. In various respects, it was both more and less difficult than what we thru-hikers were doing. However, it was unquestionably more dangerous. Many times along the way when passing through hair-raising or sketchy parts of the trail, I had remarked, "I'm damn sure glad I'm not trying to get through here on a horse."

Pepperoni didn't have any kids, and these two horses had been her pride and joy. I couldn't help but thinking that she was going through some guilt-ridden angst over what had happened. But she really wasn't reckless. After all, she had turned around back at snowy Forrester's Pass and re-traced the two previous days of riding to find a safer route.

Then there was Ralph. Our first introduction to Ralph had been when he—over a point of honor concerning his wife not being assisted while stranded one day—had threatened to kill the husband of the other woman attempting to thru-ride the PCT.

"I'll blow his head off," he had screamed repeatedly in a red-faced rage. "And I'll be raising my hands in triumph for the cameras when they lead me into the courtroom."

We hadn't known what to think of him. Apparently, the object of his fusillade hadn't either. The man had fled back to Arkansas, where he had put out word on the internet that a dangerous madman was loose on the PCT. The God's honest truth, though, is that the more you saw of Ralph, the more you realized he wouldn't hurt a flee. His biggest problem, as far as I could see, was that he would do absolutely anything for anybody. This left him totally at a loss over how to understand somebody like the other husband, who was a man of means and wouldn't go out of his way for others.

"I can only imagine what Ralph is going through right now, given his emotional nature," several people commented. The tone was one of unmistakable affection. Ralph had gone from trail freak to a trail favorite.

"I had been looking forward to seeing them when they passed us going south," Whiskey Jet said.

"Yeah, I thought about that too," others said.

The amazing thing, though, is that we hadn't seen the last of them. Pepperoni would soon dust herself off, arrange for more horses, and continue south. As the ancient Greeks said, character is fate.

***

The arid terrain continued to amaze me. We passed the length of the rim of Crater Lake the following morning gazing continuously into its heavenly blue waters. Yet the area for the next forty or fifty miles was dry as a bone despite also receiving *44 feet* of precipitation per year. I couldn't understand it. Was the intensity of the summertime sun so that it dries out the soil that quickly?

A trail angel resolved our plight with dozens of containers of water stashed where the PCT crosses Highway 138. The following day in the middle of a long dry stretch, Uber Bitch found us another diversionary route along a series of lakes. I was getting used to drinking this lake water, but it wasn't something to savor. A lot of the day I simply had a feeling of low-level thirstiness.

Finally, we came to the McKenzie Highway. Uber Bitch and I had planned to hitch from here to the thriving trail town of Sisters, Oregon.

"Hey, why don't we go on and hike the 17 miles today to Santiam Pass?' Uber Bitch said.

"Yeah," I said unenthusiastically. "We could do that."

Meanwhile, a lot of the hikers who had boasted they were going to hike all the way to Santiam Pass today, got off 17 miles early and hitched into Sisters from the McKenzie Highway so they could get the alcohol flowing early. Better (or worse) yet, many of them never did the seventeen miles. When they left Sisters a couple days later with various degrees of hangovers, they hitched back to the trail 17 miles north at Santiam Pass. Perhaps our parents were right, after all, about seeking good influences.

The problem, though, was that this seventeen miles was hellish. I couldn't believe my eyes.

"The trail goes over that?" I said in disbelief.

"Yeah," Uber Bitch said. "Those are lava beds from another volcano explosion."

It felt like a heat furnace as we strained to pick from one charred, lava-formed rock to another in the mid-day sun.

The endless varieties of terrain on the PCT is staggering.

There should have been some alien-planet novelty to the whole experience. But I was thirsty and exhausted, and barely spoke another word the rest of the day. This time I was the one struggling to keep up with Uber Bitch. Finally, we made it to Santiam Pass where her husband was waiting to take us in to Sisters.

Hiking should be about something other than miles. But, let's face it, sometimes that's exactly what it's all about. Uber Bitch and I had hiked 288 miles in twelve days. That had it's own feeling of fulfillment, and I was a little bit proud of myself upon reaching Sisters (an always dangerous feeling!)

It was now September 1st, and we had 650 miles to get Canada. It had seemed unlikely I could make it there before the October 1st recommended guideline. But now it seemed doable, if only Uber Bitch and I could keep up our inexorable pace. If only.

Chapter 36

66 Hours

What could break our seemingly unstoppable momentum? The most unlikely things.

It was the Friday before Labor Day weekend, and the perfect day to hike. I had been looking forward to seeing lots of Oregonian outdoor-types gamely taking to the woods for the holiday weekend. Unfortunately, in the first fourteen miles, diarrhea chased me to the bushes at least once an hour.

Finally, we arrived at Rockpile Lake, which, with its bucolic, serene setting, presented a scene out of Norman Rockwell America.

"Unfortunately, I'm gonna' have to call it a day," I said to Uber Bitch.

"Well, this looks like as good of a place as any," she agreed, and we pitched our tents on the far side of the lake *for the night*. That was nice of her, because she was in an especial hurry. She missed her husband terribly; it appeared to be that rare happy marriage. Apparently, he had labeled her Uber Bitch because of a rush of surliness that had overcome her when she had given up caffeine in preparation for this hike.

But a hiker is like an army; we move on our stomachs. My stomach was turning somersaults and not going anywhere. *Do I have Giardia?* This intestinal disease is the dread of even the most intrepid of long-distance hikers; it often seemed like luck of the draw who got it.

Giggles, who had already gotten Giardia twice, passed by.

When he saw what was up, he immediately pronounced, "You've got Giardia, Skywalker. You need some antibiotics." But I wasn't convinced, although I did have to rush out of my tent a few more times in the evening. *Am I going to be able to hike tomorrow?*

"How are you feeling?" Uber Bitch asked when I got out of my tent at first light.

"Better," I said, and began packing up my backpack. I even dabbled in another crummy hiker breakfast.

"I'm gonna' start slow," I told her, "and try to catch you mid-day."

"Is there anything I can do for you?"

"No, it should be alright."

Off she went. I never saw her again.

The beautiful weather of the day before had given way to heavy cloud cover. It started raining. I used my stomach and the rain as an excuse to unpack my backpack and re-erect my tent. There I was to lay for the next 54 hours.

***

Sitting in a tent listening to the pitter-patter of rain can be one of life's pleasures. Or it can be like the ninth circle of Dante's inferno. Depends on the circumstances. In this case, my initial comfort was diminished by guilt. *I told her I was going to catch up with her.* Guilt ended up being the least of my problems, however. Unsurprisingly, cold weather did. And boredom. Unlike many hikers, I didn't carry a book because I was so weight sensitive.

I was bolstered when the familiar faces of Carhartt (hiked in Carhartts) and Not a Chance arrived late on the first afternoon. Carhartt was an Iraqi veteran of the stiff upper-lip variety. He stubbornly refused to believe he couldn't start a fire, and practically set an entire stump on fire to prove it. It was a fabulous relief, and greatly reduced my shivering before I got in my tent. However, I had become 'sleep greedy', and made a basic mistake in setting up my tent. In wet weather, it is always best to erect your tent on an incline so that the water will rush past it. But I had set mine up in a flat spot. Water was able to gather underneath the tent and easily penetrate its fabric. My down sleeping bag became soaked. Down, of course, is the cat's meow of fabrics; that is, until it gets wet.

Bitter cold weather doesn't usually lead to hypothermia. Cold and wet, however, is the perfect recipe. By morning I was both, and desperate to get the hell out of there. But there was one big problem. The weather had gotten a helluva' lot worse overnight. It never was to get over forty degrees all day with heavy gusts of wind tearing across the lake. I knew only two things: I wasn't going anywhere today, and this was potentially dangerous.

Finally, in the early afternoon Rocket Man jumped out of his tent and—God bless him—attempted to show some leadership. "I'm gonna' set up a line between two trees and we can put these wet sleeping bags up to dry, and get a fire going." That gave me a glimmer of hope, and I emerged from my tent for the first time. But it quickly became obvious it was all useless. The rain and wind got worse, and Rocket Man retreated to the safety of his tent.

Carhartt had actually headed out to hike in the morning. Knowing him, he was either going to make some decent miles or die. Not a Chance, like so many, was infatuated with Carhartt's bluff style. She had tried heading out too. However, she soon turned back and by the time she reached our campsite was shivering uncontrollably. Her tent had leaked even worse than mine last night and her sleeping bag was drenched.

"I need somebody to share body warmth with," she said simply. Fifteen feet away, ensconced in his tent, was Five Dollar, with whom she had struck up such a torrid romance with back in the desert. However, it had been of the high-passion, high-conflict variety. Alas, conflict had won out. The relationship had been reduced to screaming matches in front of the hiking community and hate mail left along the trail ("Five Dollar eats live golden retriever puppies.")

So Five Dollar was out. Instead, she went to Leprechaun's tent and asked if she could get in. Leprechaun was a Georgia mountain boy who spoke with a slow drawl; but you'd have sworn he was a New Yorker he accepted so fast. There was nothing diabolical about this. Dealing with bad weather was the art of the possible.

They had to move his tent in the middle of the night it got so swamped with water.

It wasn't going to be possible for me to sleep tonight. Nor was it going to be possible to stay dry. I had one overriding mission—avoid the *Big H*. In fact, I probably already had a case of the *mild H*, but I knew from past experience that a person could recover from that. I had on eight layers up top (two sets of long-johns, hiking shirt, desert shirt, wind shirt, fleece, down vest, and marmot jacket) and three layers on the bottom. Because my sleeping bag was a wet rag, I put it over me, instead of getting in it. My socks were wet, so I decided to keep my wet shoes on. *I'm not gonna' panic. I'm gonna make it.*

Then the weather took an unexpected turn—for the worse, yet again. Torrential storms ripped at the flaps of my tent, and I began to wonder if it might blow down altogether. The leaking in the tent became rivulets coursing in various directions through the tent. I changed positions from the left side, to the right side, to my back about every half-hour. Each time I would see just how much water had accumulated on each side. It was spilling over my *Z-Rest* sleeping pad. Soon, I would be lying in a puddle. *I need to get out of here.*

Where can I go? I damn sure couldn't disturb Not a Chance and Leprechaun, unless I was really at death's door. Giggles and Rocket Man were nearby. Both had done a sporty job of setting up their tarps to avoid water runoff. But both were tight fits, with no room for an extra body of even average size.

That left only one option—Five Dollar. On a personal basis, it was by far the most embarrassing. He was very unusual to begin with. He had grown up a Mormon, but had harshly rejected the religion. I had periodically scrimmaged with him over this (Five Dollar—"They're all a bunch of crooks." Me— "You can't condemn ten million people in such a general way.") But for the most part, we had gotten along well. In fact, along the way we had gotten in the habit of swapping jokes about the 'inflatables' that we both claimed to be carrying in our backpacks, as well as other perverted humor. It was all par for the course. But the prospect of now having to approach his tent in the middle of the night and beg him to let me in was mortifying. However, this situation of getting wetter and colder by the minute was ominous. I was desperate.

I don't want to do it. But you've got to do it. I don't want to do it. You have to. This is a once in a lifetime emergency. He will understand.

But I desperately didn't want to do it. *Try something else.* I began doing deep-breathing exercises, and alternated stretching exercises for various parts of the body. I normally kept my backpack and food bag in the vestibule of the tent, if only to keep a little distance between me and a bear that might steal my food bag. I grabbed the backpack and moved it into the tent as a headrest, and resolved to periodically eat some snacks.

Finally, the storm climaxed and its intensity began to abate. *What time is it?* I didn't have a watch, but spent the next few hours trying to guess the time and hoping to divine the first ray of light. At least it kept me thinking, which is critical in avoiding hypothermia. Slowly, the sun came up and the rain completely died off.

I didn't even get out of my tent until about 10 or 11 o'clock. Continuing north on the PCT was out of the question. I needed new gear—a tent that didn't leak, a synthetic sleeping bag instead of a down bag, and some new gloves. Not a Chance was in even more dire straits than me, and we separately re-traced the fourteen miles back to Sisters.

There, I called Uber Bitch's husband to explain why I hadn't kept up with his wife. To my surprise, he put me on the phone with *her*. She had found a steep side trail during the ferocious second day of storm and called her husband to pick her off.

"I'm off the trail," she said heavily. "Sorry."

"No worries," I said. "But I'll sure as heck miss you as a hiking partner."

I then hitched to Bend, Oregon, where the only REI was located. *What a stroke of luck to have this problem in the only place where there is a nearby REI.* Lucky, that is, unless you just happen to be in the near 7-foot range. Then they will tell you that you are SOL (....out of luck). They didn't have a single tent I could fit in, nor did they have a 7-foot down or synthetic sleeping bag. I did pick up some new gloves and an emergency space blanket.

But for the most part, I was gonna' have to make it to Canada with what I had. This whole Labor Day weekend debacle effectively cost me four precious days and God-knows-how-much weight. The possibility of very cold, wet weather would occupy me to the point of obsession from here on out. Even on nice, sunny days, it would be in the back of my mind—the clock is ticking up there in northern Washington.

Chapter 37

Pretty Boy Joe

The PCT is not a pioneer experience. Don't get me wrong. It's a very demanding challenge for the average person such as myself. But the U.S. Forest Service and dedicated trail volunteers have done an admirable job of maintaining the trail, and good maps are generally available. We know exactly when we're gonna' hit trail towns along the way to stock up on food.

However, as I covered large parts of the West, I couldn't help but wonder if amongst the trail population were a few folks who would have made kindred souls with the likes of Davy Crocket, Kit Carson, or Daniel Boone back in the 19th century. Almost surely, the answer is yes.

My favorite candidate would probably be *Pretty Boy Joe*. He was 22 years old, just graduated from the University of California, and chock full of idealism. However, he seemed to have a maturity well beyond his years, and got along well with the trail's more senior citizens (such as myself). With his long, lean physique, straight gaze, and manner of speaking in the soft, unhurried cadences of the West, he even reminded me of a younger Clint Eastwood.

His hiking style was utterly unpredictable. From the very beginning to the very end, I'd see him turn up at all odd times of the day and evening, and from all kinds of side trails. Back in the desert, he had found a dead rattlesnake on the trail, skinned it, and carried it draping off his backpack for weeks. Then, he had met a Dartmouth University student out for summer hikes; soon

One of the less pretty faces of Pretty Boy Joe. This talented 22-year-old often seemed afflicted with a low boredom threshold.

the two of them were performing dumpster dives. It wasn't for financial necessity, as Joe's father was reputedly a very wealthy California real estate maven.

"I hate seeing things go to waste," he simply said.

Luna had given him his trail name, and other women had commented excitedly on this tall, handsome prince. But he proved to be quite elusive. Surely, he wasn't immune to temptation. However, the more I saw of him the more I saw a larger force at work.

"We Americans are titillated by sex, obsessed by it, horrified by it, wrote Jon Krakauer in *Into the Wild*. "When an apparently healthy young man, elects to forgo the enticements of the flesh, suspicions are aroused."

Krakauer mentioned Thoreau (who reputedly died a virgin), John Muir, and Tolstoy—as well as the book's protagonist, Chris McCandless—as adventurers and intellectuals who maintained ambivalent attitudes towards sex. "Like not a few of those seduced by the wild, McCandless seems to have been driven by a variety of lust that supplanted sexual desire. His yearning, in a sense, was too powerful to be quenched by human contact."

Pretty Boy Joe seemed to have similar impulses at work. He sought a more ecstatic way of living; comfort and security were secondary. In fact, we chatted six months after the PCT hike ended and he told me he had been eating out of dumpsters at least every other day (Having worked in a retirement home and seen how much food they throw away, I recommended he look for some 'geriatric dumpsters').

***

"This Timberline Lodge tests the workability of recreational facilities built by the government itself and operated under its complete control," Franklin Delano Roosevelt said on September 28, 1937 at its dedication.

Like a lot of people, I have been infected at times with the prejudice that our federal government seemingly can't do anything right. However, one trip to a place like Timberline Lodge utterly refutes that notion. It's a classic case of something that simply wouldn't have gotten done if the government hadn't done it.

It's brilliantly done by the famed depression-era WPA. Hundreds of out-of-work artisans employed by the WPA did the Lodge up with Native American materials and in western motifs. The rustic design had a subliminal appeal to my simple tastes. After an extensive tour of the lodge, I went so far as to vow, "If I ever get married, this is where the honeymoon happens."

The lodge is actually only halfway up Mount Hood, at about the point tree-line is breached. That had been plenty OK with me, given the mountain has seen over 130 deaths in the last centry – most having to do with sudden weather change (In one notorious case in May, 1986, fourteen high school students were killed when the teacher urged the group to keep climbing in a snowstorm. The class was a requirement, not an elective). However, Pretty Boy Joe had seemed disappointed. As we had started up Mount Hood that morning, Joe had spotted some ski slopes.

"I'm going up there," he said non-chalantly, and off he had gone.

My immediate purpose at Timberline Lodge was very straightforward—to commit mayhem at the buffet. For the very reasonable (given the magnitude of what is getting ready to transpire) price of $16, one gets the choice of all manner of delicatessens and delights. In fact, my five helpings there may have been my five best meals on the entire PCT. Others said the same. And this comes from people who at times revere food to the point of sac-religion.

Pretty Boy Joe finally turned up after a steep climb up a glacier field. Along the way he had picked up a Danish hiker named *Valhalla*. "This place is really cool," Joe said in his soft-spoken manner, and then went poking around looking for some nook or cranny where he could hide for the night.

"How about this?" he said to Valhalla and me, as he perched up in what looked like a small attic or linen closet.

That pretty much left Valhalla and me to hike out from Timberline Lodge at dusk. And we were to stay pretty much together the rest of the way.

***

"Scandinavians are navigators," Valhalla plainly said. "Look at the Vikings. It runs in our blood."

Over the years I have cottoned on to the contrarian notion that being from a small country has great advantages.

"The Danes are everybody's favorite travelers," my roommate in a Latin American hostel once spontaneously said. He may have been on to something. To that you could probably add the Swiss and the New Zealanders. These people from modest-sized countries aren't afflicted with all these silly, megalomaniacal arguments—"We're the biggest, the best, the most sophisticated—that we Americans, French, and British like to scrimmage over.

Their secret is they adapt. Valhalla was 50 years old and in trim form. As I got to know him better, it became clear he had traveled absolutely everywhere, despite making a modest salary as a social worker. Obviously, he knew how to do more with less. That's kinda' what hiking is all about.

He was also a map-reader *non-pareil*. This skill came in quite handy right off the bat, in the confusing maze of circuitous routes above tree line.

"Hey, we can take this side trail to Ramona Falls," he said enthusiastically.

"Yeah, I guess," I answered unenthusiastically, thinking about the extra miles it would add. To be sure, it was spectacular as we entered a lush green forest and soon came upon water rushing over a volcanic cliff. But Canada was still a helluva' long way away.

"I don't think it will be that cold up there in October," Valhalla said. Of course, being Scandinavian, he would say that.

Pretty Boy Joe had bolted from Timberline Lodge at 6 a.m., and soon caught up with us with tales of his previous night's evasive activities. I had forsworn night-hiking just a few nights before. But the odds of these two characters stopping at any reasonable hour were slim. At dark, we found ourselves on an exposed ridge in a steady drizzle, which conjured up deep-seated fears. Fortunately, Valhalla located what appeared to be an obscure side trail for us to camp. That side trail ended up being the most spectacular short-distance trail in the Northwest.

The Eagle Creek Trail is an engineering marvel. Over the course of just twenty miles, it passes a half-dozen major waterfalls. WPA workers had blasted ledges out of sheer cliffs for hikers to walk along (with clammy palms, to be sure!). In one place they had even smashed an entire tunnel out of a rock wall, so that hikers can walk underneath a 150 foot waterfall called Tunnel Falls. That was exhilarating enough for me. But not for Pretty Boy Joe. Soon he found a way down a steep bank, and suddenly had stripped down and dove naked in the pool of water where the cascades were crashing down.

It was a Sunday afternoon and the Eagle Creek Trail was teeming with weekend hikers coming up from the Columbia River Gorge. That's where we were headed down to. We lost over 4,000 feet of elevation as we descended towards the gorge in what proved to be a glorious end to Oregon. Practically every hiker had developed an affinity for this state, so populated with adventurous souls.

We arrived at the small, riverside town of Cascade Locks, which at 150 feet is the lowest point on the entire PCT. The town was hospitable enough to allow hikers to camp and shower for free in a city park right along the river. Washington State—where I had never set foot—lay just across the way. But it was this magnificent Colombia River lying right in front of us that I couldn't get my mind off.

It was one of the scenes in what I still consider, even in this day and age of revisionist history, to be one of the most dramatic stories of the American epic. I speak, of course, of *the Corps of Discovery.*

Chapter 38

The Corps of Discovery

The library of Thomas Jefferson is the stuff of legend. With 15,000 volumes, it was by far the largest collection of books in the country. Better yet, Jefferson seemed to have actually read most of them. His collection on North American geography was unparalleled anywhere in the world. There was one book in this collection, however, that had captured his imagination more than any other. In fact, he had become virtually obsessed by it.

The book was entitled *Voyages from Montreal, Through the Continent of North America, to the Pacific Ocean*. It was written by a young Scotsman named Alexander Mackenzie. In 1793, MacKenzie had attempted to find a continual water route all the way to the Pacific Ocean. MacKenzie's crew had navigated various waterways from Montreal, Canada all the way to the Canadian Rockies. There his team found a mountain pass with an elevation of only 3,000 feet to get over the Rockies. They were easily able to portage (carry their boat overland) at this mountain pass, and eventually made it to the Pacific. There he staked a British claim to the Northwest. This alarmed Jefferson.

One specific passage in the book was particularly provocative. MacKenzie described the Columbia as "the most Northern situation fit for colonization, and suitable to the residence of a civilized people." His recommended solution was for the British to settle the Columbia River. The possibility of the British moving south and colonizing the Columbia River threw the normally self-contained Jefferson into manic activity.

Thomas Jefferson was probably the greatest *Francophile*, and the greatest *Anglophobe*, in American history. This was especially ironic in a country that tends to be just the opposite. However, amongst the Nation's Founders, suspicion of the British ran universally deep. Despite losing their thirteen colonies on the Atlantic coast in the Revolutionary War, Great Britain still held more land on the American continent than the United States. When Jefferson took the oath of office as President in 1801, he had every intention of reversing this.

What followed, of course, was the Louisiana Purchase. The seller, Napoleon Bonaparte, couldn't believe his luck. Why would we actually pay for the territory? After all, France was bogged down in the Napoleonic Wars with England, and had no way to defend the territories from the United States.

"The sale gives England a rival," he chortled.

The situation in the American West was like a chessboard—extremely fluid. To be sure, the European imperial powers were veterans at power politics and land grabbing. What they couldn't reckon on, however, was that Jefferson, the notorious Romantic Man of the Enlightenment, would prove to be quite the Machiavellian, himself.

***

One huge question had been just how wide the American continent was—2,000, 3,000, 5,000 miles? Nobody had known for sure until British Captain James Cook's third voyage up the Pacific Coast in 1780. The information from this voyage gave Jefferson a rough idea of the extent of the American continent. It was about 3,000 miles wide.

Jefferson and his secretary and alter-ego, Merriwether Lewis had picked up some vague information from various Indians passing through Washington about a large mountain chain in the West. Their best guess was that these mountains (the Rockies) were probably about the same height and breadth as the Appalachian Mountain Chain. Thus, Lewis shouldn't have too much trouble finding a route to the Pacific. They even thought Lewis' expedition could sail to and from the Pacific in one year.

This was in spite of the fact that both of them thought woolly mammoths and other prehistoric creatures stalked the West.

The general belief was that the Louisiana Purchase covered the area between the Mississippi River and the Continental Divide. However, Jefferson had a more expansive interpretation—that it also included the Northwest Territories on the far side of the Continental Divide. It was up for grabs. But he needed an all-water Northwest Passage to stake an American claim. The Russians were known to have designs on a warm water ports in the Northwest region. The Spanish, who then held California, were perennial candidates to grab the Oregon territories further north. But the greatest threat was the British.

Jefferson's and Lewis' competitive instincts were aroused. If the British had already done it, we could do it better. This expedition was destined to be American naivete at its best.

***

It's tempting, but I'm not going to go into the details of Lewis and Clark's famous journey. The story is told in spellbinding fashion by Stephen Ambrose in his bestseller, *Undaunted Courage.*

However, a few points do seem noteworthy:

--Lewis and Clark operated the Corps of Discovery through a joint command. Traditionally, this has had disastrous effects on a military mission. Why did it work here? The two men trusted each other completely. Never once did they quarrel.

--They had the very best men and equipment of the time on the mission. Every frontiersman, mapmaker, hunter, fisherman, woodsman, or boat builder worth his salt was dying for the opportunity to go west on this historic mission. Eventually, 33 people were named by Lewis and Clark. They chose well. Only one member died, and that was from sickness.

--No tales, of course, can match the drama of Sacagawea, the Shoshone Indian girl who helped get them safely through the Rockies. However, Cameahwait, Old Toby, and other Indians also guided them at critical junctures. Lewis and Clark deserve credit for having a gut-level feel for just whom they could trust.

--President Jefferson, as well as Lewis and Clark, had generally enlightened attitudes toward natives. "Treat them in the most friendly manner which their own conduct will permit," were Jefferson's instructions. He had every intention of constructively bringing them into the American orbit. Only sporadic violence was perpetrated along the way against the native tribes, and it was generally done in self-defense. Unfortunately, neither Jefferson (a large slaveowner), Lewis, nor Clark showed such high-mindedness towards blacks. Clark brought a slave (York) along who participated fully in Corps activities. But Clark treated him very differently from the other men, and refused York's request for release upon return.

***

In a technical sense, the Lewis and Clark mission was a failure. They didn't find an all-water route to link the Atlantic with the Pacific that Jefferson so badly wanted. But what they did achieve was ultimately more important. Their journey firmly staked an American claim not just on the territory explicitly acquired in the Louisiana Purchase, but the territory west of the Rocky Mountains as well.

The British were still much more powerful than the United States and could easily have extended their territorial claims down to the Columbia River. The headwaters of the Columbia lie several hundred miles north in the Canadian Rockies, which would have made this huge river a more natural border.

Given that the PCT is a hike from Mexico to Canada, I would now be finished if that alternative scenario had prevailed. Part of me would have been relieved at that prospect. However, the PCT in Washington combines great beauty with difficulty. With a certain amount of trepidation, to be sure, I was greatly looking forward to it.

Chapter 39

The Evergreen State

Without perpetual uncertainty,
the drama of human life would be destroyed.

Winston Churchill

"You know you're supposed to buy all of your food for Washington in Cascade Locks," Uber Bitch had told me back in central Oregon.

"You're honestly telling me there's not one decent grocery store we're going to pass in all of Washington," I had protested.

"Forget it. There's nothing there." Other hikers confirmed it.

"I'm gonna' hike all the way through Washington without spending a dime," Pretty Boy Joe immediately announced.

"What, are you gonna' re-enact the Donner's Pass episode?" I responded. But, of course, he was serious, as we would soon see.

The rest of us mortals, though, had a critical planning calculation to make. We had to buy all the food we would need for the next 500 miles here in Cascade Locks. Adding to the complication was the fact that the grocery store here in Cascade Locks wasn't very large. Actually, I had always found that wandering through grocery stores in trail towns was a bit of an unnerving experience. Decisions you make in there will have direct tangible effects on your physical persona and morale a few days hence. The first 2,000 miles had worked out pretty well. I had cut it close plenty of times, but never completely run out of food.

On second thought, however, maybe it hadn't worked out so well. I was down 45 pounds from my initial starting weight of 213. *How big of a problem is this?*

"When you start smelling something like ammonia, you know you're burning muscle," one hiker had told me back in California. That had sounded just too strange to be convincing. However, a few hundred miles back, I had indeed begun emitting an ammonia-like odor that, even in my most narcissistic state, wasn't very fond of myself.

Now, I joined other hikers scurrying around fretting over just how much food to send. The grocery store didn't have everything I wanted, which meant improvising. Eventually, I spent $300 on just about the most boilerplate food you could imagine, including 28 packs of Idahoan potatoes.

A matter of hot debate amongst hikers was which post offices to send food shipments to in Washington State. After much agonizing, I sent out food drops to four places: White Pass, and to the post offices at Snoqualmie, Skykomish, and Stehekin (If you don't think the Indians have any grievances, take another look at those names!).

Valhalla, however, harbored the general European prejudice against American over-consumption, especially overeating. He was betting that food would appear somewhere in this food-crazy country.

"I'm not sending any food drops," he declared. "I refuse to believe there is anywhere in America where there is not a lot of food." He later ended up having to 'borrow' some food from me.

Valhalla, Pretty Boy Joe, and I then dodged traffic in both directions as we crossed the densely-girdered *Bridge of the Gods* that led over the Columbia River and into Washington State.

***

Oregon's speedway quickly gave way to steeper, more jagged terrain. Autumn offered brilliant hues and bracing air. Our food bags were full and I had good hiking partners, as the northern cascade range loomed ahead. It was all perfect. *Pleeeeez hold off, old man winter.*

Within three days we had gone from 150 feet sea level to back up over 7,000 feet at Goat Rocks Wilderness. The sharply angular mountains and bleak landscape immediately brought to mind the White Mountains in New Hampshire. At turns, I found myself ecstatic and horrified. On the way up to the crest we came upon yet another glacier that required tortuously slow walking. It seemed so simple, yet was so icy. It didn't take a great imagination to envision sliding helplessly hundreds of yards before careening into a backstop of rocks.

Fortunately, CanaDoug was a day behind. He always got this gleeful Canadian joy out of demonstrating his alpine prowess, and then lighting up a cigar and watching me flail awkwardly through snow and ice. Again I managed to make it through another glacier field, although my technique (deep crouch and claw for a grip) wasn't getting any more aesthetically pleasing.

We wound and wound around to the top and beheld one of the great views on the Pacific Crest Trail. To me, singular views are somewhat overrated. The more profound experience is to walk through nature and subconsciously embrace its holistic majesty. But the view from the crest of Goats Rock Wilderness, with its sharp spine running along for miles between deep canyons and snow-capped peaks in the distance, was one for the ages.

Luna, my tormentor, but ultimately my inspiration, on Mount Whitney was on hand to enjoy it. She now had a new hiking partner. Like a lot of the girls I've seen on hiking trails, Luna was a pretty good 'picker'. She had traveled long distances with two older guys who had practically maimed themselves struggling to keep up with her. Both had been on their best behavior, but 500 miles seemed to be about the shelf life of her tolerance for these followers. At that point they helplessly became *personas non-grata*.

What had happened was pretty simple and, if you think about it, forgivable. In Oregon, Luna had gotten what movie director, Spike Lee, might call 'jungle fever'. She had sprung for what was probably the most impressive physical specimen of male out here. That was 21 year-old Waffles from rural Tennessee— he of the long hair and ripped physique. Luna was a handful, to be sure. But Waffles had the confidence to fill the vacuum. However, other hikers suddenly began blowing a lot of flak his way. Unfortunately, he occasionally used the *n-word*, which opened him up for all kinds of condemnation. As a southerner, I'm always sensitive when a fellow southerner exposes his horns this way.

"Just because you're a southerner," Backtrack lectured him one day, "doesn't mean you have to be a racist."

Regrettably, I also had used this nefarious word on occasion while growing up. So I was in no position to lecture him, and actually got along with him pretty well. In reality, I thought there was a more basic reason Waffles was drawing fire from his colleagues.

He had scored with Luna and they hadn't.

***

Valhalla and I came to a bluff described in our guidebook as *bleak alpine campsites*. They couldn't have described it more appropriately.

"I think I'll camp here and walk around taking photographs," the sophisticated aesthete announced.

"I'd never be able to stay warm here," I said. "Plus I need to make more miles." With that, I headed off as fast as I could.

The best thing to do when alone is to hike. With the mindset I was in, it was inevitable I was going to hike until dark almost any day. A half-hour before dark, I would start actively looking for places to camp. But then I would get 'mileage greedy'. Whenever I spotted a decent camp spot in the next twenty minutes, I would briefly hesitate before saying to myself, five more minutes. Hikers frequently lamented, "Every morning after I turn the first corner, I come right on a spot that would have been perfect." The moral of the story, according to thru-hikers anyway, was to eke out every last minute of daylight until the perfect spot presented itself. But the law of averages also says you're going to get caught in some awful places to camp with this mentality.

As dark descended here, I knew I was in an unfortunate area. After dropping sharply from Goats Rock Pass, the trail had then ascended 1,600 feet. Now I was stuck on top of a narrow ridge without tree cover or any possibility of a flat spot. I was also bone-tired, not having seen a trail town for almost a hundred miles. The only thing to do, though, was get back below tree line. Fast.

It became spooky dark, but I finally got back below tree line. I was very aware that this is the type situation that one is likely to have a surprise encounter with a wild animal. I kept banging my ski pole loudly on trees, and singing an atonal version of Otis Redding's Sittin' on the *Dock of the Bay*. Finally, after going my maximum speed in the pitch black dark for about an hour, the trail came to the bottom of an undulation. There wasn't anywhere wide enough to throw down a tent. So I just lay down on my sleeping bag and pad in the middle of the trail.

But that's where some animals often prefer to take nighttime excursions. That keen awareness marred my night's sleep. Valhalla, meanwhile, had enjoyed a blissful alpine afternoon, gotten a good night's sleep, and soon caught up with my dragging *keisters* on the trail the next day. In this instance, at least, his less frantic European style had proven more adept than my more grasping American attitude.

***

"Man, what's happened to you?" Dirk said.

"What do you mean?" I laughed.

"Where did the rest of you go?"

We had by chance run into each other at the country store at White Pass, where everybody was inhaling containers of ice cream and bartering parts of our food packages we had all picked up here.

These impromptu observations were standard trail fare. You would see somebody you hadn't seen in a couple weeks—in some cases just a few days—and immediately notice part of them had wasted away. Unfortunately, I seemed to be on the receiving end of a disproportionate number of these remarks.

I honestly didn't feel like this large-scale weight loss had affected my actual hiking, except for late in the afternoon when a persistent fatigue would set in. Its major effect lay in loss of insulation and ability to stay warm. My arm muscles had atrophied, and any chest, stomach, and shoulder mass had wasted away.

"That's scary," Poet had unhesitatingly said when she saw me changing shirts at a campsite way back in northern California. And the problem had only gotten more acute since then. In fact, it was reaching the stage where I was finally ready to play a *wild card*.

All along the Appalachian Trail, and now on the PCT, concerned fellow hikers had suggested in low voices, "Have you ever tried olive oil? It's absolutely packed with calories."

It sounded awful. Nonetheless, I had filed it away mentally as a last resort when nothing else worked. Now that time had come with a vengeance. At Cascade Locks, I had sent a container of olive oil here to White Pass. Despite weighing just a few ounces, it contained almost 4,000 calories. I threw it into my backpack.

I tried to view it like taking an asthma shot—something unpleasant I had to do. From here on out, I didn't take a bite out of anything without lathering it with olive oil. I was pleasantly surprised. I had expected it to be absolutely horrible, but it was merely bad. Better yet, I could actually feel it working. It had a rich body to it that average hiker food lacks, and I immediately felt like I was gaining strength (and flatulence!).

The first thing I did at the end of the journey was weigh myself; I had lost 43 pounds, which meant I had actually gained two pounds in Washington State. Miraculous.

Chapter 40

The Northern Cascades

"The northern Cascades are the most primitive and roughest terrain in the contiguous United States," said PCT founder, Clinton Churchill Clarke. Indeed, we were leaving the more pliable southern Cascades behind, and entering a landscape of steep peaks, narrow gorges, and sharp angles cut by ice and snow.

Valhalla and I entered Rainier National Park, where the towering presence of Mount Rainier loomed off in the distance. Fortunately, the PCT designers were sane enough to not route the trail over this towering eminence. Rainier has years it actually gets up to 1,000 inches annually of snow. Its summit has

The PCT hiker draws inspiration from Mount Rainier
without actually having to risk the summit.

more glacial ice than anywhere else in the continental United States, and is completely uninhabitable by anybody not carrying technical climbing equipment (and, to be perfectly accurate, quite a few that are carrying it). But such are the vicissitudes of weather patterns in the Northwest that the eastern side of Rainier was bone dry. When Valhalla and I finally located a narrow bluff overlooking the valley to set up our tents, I had to lend him water to tide him over.

It was hunting season, and we were right in the middle of it all. It was a novelty to me for the simple reason that, despite being from Georgia, I'd never been hunting.

"What is that sound?" I asked Valhalla when we heard a high-pitched squeal. "Hear it?"

"Yeah," he laughed. "It's a, uh, I don't know how to say it in English—kind of like a moose."

Finally, we came upon two hunters at a dirt road.

"Excuse me," I asked. "Do you know what animal keeps making that buzzing sound?"

"Shhhh," he said, conspiratorially. "Elk."

"Man, that sound is really weird. It sounds like a power line malfunctioning."

"Yeah, it's mating season," one of them said.

I never got to see one—perhaps because three's a crowd this time of year—but they sounded enormous. Lewis and Clark's expeditionary members survived the winter of 1806 by shooting and devouring 131 of these elk. Hunting them looked like gut-wrenching business, but I make no moral judgments. I don't shoot them, but I've sure eaten 'em.

I doubt I've ever eaten any bear, though. Apparently people do, however. The next day at the top of a hill, we came upon two more hunters clad in dark green outfits. My morale had just been restored at the bottom of that same hill when we had passed by a pickup truck with several bottles of water lying in the back. Since I had been running low on water, I had dropped a dollar on top of the container and grabbed one of the bottles.

"Elk hunters?" I cheerfully asked the twosome.

"No," one of them answered cheerlessly. "bear."

"Oh," I raised an eyebrow. "Do you eat them?" I asked excitedly.

"Quiet." They then commenced a FBI-style interrogation of us about bears in the immediate area.

"You didn't even notice the footprints leading up the ridge back there?" one asked in disbelief.

"No."

"Well, what have you seen?" the other guy asked, getting impatient.

"Actually, we thought this was more like Big Foot country," I piped in.

My sense of humor was vastly under appreciated, and they walked away impatiently. But when I started yakking with Valhalla, I was reprimanded again for talking too loud. My stereotype of hunters had always been of gregarious, swashbuckling types. However bear hunters, at least, seem to fall in the category of humorless zealots. And boy was I glad they hadn't seen me take that bottle of water from their truck.

Valhalla and I continued through hunting country, and within a couple more days were following the trail straight down the face of some ski slopes into the small mountainous village of Snoqualmie. We were making good time and the momentum was with us. It was a magnificently clear Saturday afternoon and, as was usually the case when arriving in a trail town, morale was high. Better yet, the lone hotel had an IHOP attached to it. This meant tonight's dinner would be olive oil-free.

When we looked over at the town's lone gas station, we caught sight of Pretty Boy Joe. It appeared he had diversified his self-sustenance activities beyond dumpster dives. He was hopping around from car to car, washing their windows. We went over to chat.

"What's the matter—no dumpsters in this town?" I lamely joked.

"This is unbelievable," he laughed, with his rakish smile. "Two ladies have already given me $20 each. Another one invited me to a party at her house."

"For God's sake, follow your motto and spread the wealth," I rejoined.

Unfortunately, our buoyant moods were quickly arrested when we ran into Dirk outside the hotel.

"Have you heard the weather forecast?" he asked quietly.

"No."

"Big-time storm coming this way," he said quietly. "Gonna' last a while too." Nobody said much of anything. Our lives for the next week had just changed dramatically.

Other than wait a week, which was unfeasible this late in the hiking season, the only possible course of action was to hike out tomorrow as planned.

***

There aren't many scenes that turn me on like crowds of people heading up a steep mountain. It is especially impressive when it's a Sunday afternoon, and they could be at home in a horizontal position with the remote control in one hand and a cell phone in the other. *Perhaps the Northwest is where I belong.* People are less likely to spend a Sunday afternoon in such a helpless position.

Sunday, September 27th, 2010 was an almost lyrically beautiful day. The crisp autumn air filled my lungs with that unmatchable tangy sensation. Backtrack, Valhalla, and I started the long climb out of Snoqualmie, that we hoped would get us to Skykomish in four days. Legions of day hikers were using the occasion to hike to the top of Chikamin Pass and take in its commanding view of the northern Cascades.

Maybe I shouldn't have been so impressed, however. Once we reached the shelf, every single person except us PCT thru-hikers headed back down the mountain to their cars. Meanwhile, after stopping to admire the views, we continued north. We wouldn't see a single other hiker for days.

Weather reminds me of the stock market. When things looks the best is usually when you are on the cusp of disaster. And given that 75% of the entire glacial ice in the Lower 48 states lies between here and the Canadian border, this is an especially fickle area. Things habitually change on a dime. In fact, a few days from now a few of our trailing comrades, including CanaDoug, would be caught in deep snow drifts in this exact spot, and facing some very difficult decisions. Things quickly got complicated.

"What the hell is that?" I wondered when we cleared a hillside the next morning and saw a heavy pall of smoke blanketing the valley.

"Looks like a forest fire," Valhalla said plainly.

"Yeah," Backtrack reminded us, "remember the trail is closed here." Indeed, in Snoqualmie we had heard a section of the PCT was closed.

The Forest Service had blocked off entrance, and the signs read: **Due to forest fires the Pacific Crest National Scenic Trail is closed in this next section. Please take an alternative route.**

Western fire-fighting doctrine had been radically altered ten years back. Instead of trying to put out forest fires, firefighters now concentrate their efforts on preventing the spread of the fires. That meant that forest fires like the one ahead of us was allowed to burn itself out. It also meant that once we stepped inside the roped off area, we were fair game.

"I read on the internet that people were going this way anyway," Backtrack said. Unlike back in the northern California fires, I was in no position to bail out this time. So the three of us headed in.

The trees were burnt down to charred embers. Most worrisome, a few small fires still burned here and there. We could only hope that everything else in there was so dead, that they wouldn't conflagrate. And *dead* was the operative word. Everything about this scene was hostile to life. Downed clumps of trees littered the PCT, and presented serious obstacle courses.

"Hey, hey. Where are you going, Skywalker? This way," I heard Valhalla and Backtrack yelling, after I had run around a huge downed tree to stake out a route.

"Are you sure?" I yelled. "There is a decent trail on the other side of these trees."

"Yes," they summoned me. "This way."

Unfortunately, a few miles later we figured out that the Danish navigator and the brainy college professor had gotten it wrong, and I had been on the right track. That meant spending the next couple hours trying to relocate the PCT. At that point the heavy clouds indicated a storm was brewing. Everyone picked up their pace.

Nobody really spoke to the others for the next few hours. Anybody who took a short break got passed without even a salute. Horrible weather lay ahead in the dark, forbidding northwestern forest.

***

Things changed drastically overnight. Smoke and fire were out. Snow and ice were in. Valhalla and I took an ill-advised break on the top of Cathedral Pass, where the full force and fury of this storm began to reveal itself.

"We'd better get down from here," Valhalla agreed. However, this side of the pass had borne the full brunt of the storm, and the trail was under a thickening blanket of snow.

At the foot of Mount Daniels, we were greeted with a stream rushing off the mountain, and tumbling all the way into the valley.

"Anywhere to cross?" Valhalla inquired.

"Doesn't look like it," I mumbled. Into the frozen stream we went to cross last year's snow melt in the new year's snow.

Once over, Valhalla pulled out his map and began intently searching for alternative routes. I was accustomed to him saying, "Oh, here. Look at this", at which point we would begin down some obscure trail. He did find a couple alternatives; however, none offered a hope of getting out of this bitter cold weather today. So I stayed glued to Valhalla's heels as we continued on in the *white silence*.

Finally, we came to a campsite well short of where we had planned on making it for the day.

"Big climb ahead," Valhalla said.

"Yeah, this looks okay for tonight," I answered, uncharacteristically pithily. After the leaking tent disaster back in Oregon, I knew what not to do—look for a flat spot. I commenced scouring the area for a moderate incline, and then set up my tent.

Right at dark, I was surprised to hear a familar voice.

"Is this it?" the person non-chalantly said. There was really only one person it could have been. Pretty Boy Joe. It was almost like the means justified the ends with this guy. Every other hiker on the PCT was surely hunkered down as safely as possible, wherever they had found to pitch their tent. Even Joe seemed to take this weather seriously, as he quickly disappeared into his hastily erected tent.

What followed was white-out conditions. All night. My tent leaked. All night. *It's got to lighten up.* But I kept hearing channels of wind originating from seemingly miles away and gathering intensity as heavier and heavier snowflakes collided into my tent.

Snowy morning finally arrived.

"So long guys," from Pretty Boy Joe was the first thing I heard.

When I emerged from my tent, Valhalla quietly said, "We need to get out of here."

"There'll be even more snow up higher?" I reminded him.

"I'll find some trail," he stoutly said. I hurried to get ready; following him was my best hope of getting out of here.

I knew it would be impossible to get my tent even remotely dry. But at least I could shake the heaviest snow off to lighten it up some. But when I began flailing it around in all directions one of the hooks accidentally banged up against my middle finger, just as had happened in Yosemite. Blood began flowing freely.

Frozen fingers, blood, and high elevations. *Damn, damn. Bad karma?* I rifled through my first aid kit and extracted several band-aids. Valhalla impatiently stood by watching me awkwardly try to wrap band-aids around the flowing wound with my biting cold fingers. It wasn't even close. The band-aids quickly overflowed. I threw them onto the snow and desperately tried wrapping more band-aids around the thin slit. But again, bright red blood overwhelmed the contraption. Panic.

"Have you got any tape?" I asked Valhalla.

"No."

It could take me an hour to get this wound clotted. Heck, it might not ever shut, and I could die in a pile of blood and snow.

Yeah, it sounds even more improbable than it does gruesome. But I honestly didn't know how in the world I was going to stop the blood from cascading out of this tiny cut in my finger. *How long can I survive bleeding freely?*

"I'm gonna' get moving, Skywalker," Valhalla said.

Oh no.

I quickly looked at him and asked, "Could you just hang around for a few minutes?"

The hiking community is highly oriented towards offering help; hardly anybody ever asks for it. In fact, I would have to say directly asking a fellow hiker to stay with me was the single lowest point for me on either the Appalachian Trail or the Pacific Crest Trail. But god-dammit, I was doing my best. And I didn't want to bleed to death or get lost in a heavy snowstorm.

"Okay," he quietly said to my request.

The Mexican guy in Yosemite had used a pad and taped it tightly down. I rifled through my first aid kit. Thank God there was a small spool of tape that had been in my first-aid kit for thousands of miles. Who knew how clean it was, but it was the only arrow in my quiver. Unartfully, I was able to tie it several times around my fingers. Unlike with the band-aids, blood didn't immediately appear.

"You ready?" Valhalla asked.

"Yeah." Off we headed to a higher elevation and deeper snow.

Regardless of who the hiker was, there could be only one possible goal today. Get the hell out of this snow and cold. That wasn't going to be possible on the actual PCT route. It was twenty miles over impassable amounts of snow. So we needed a shortcut.

"There's got to be another way," Valhalla said intently.

I followed intently on his heels. *Economy of motion. Don't give out.*

"This looks like the Surprise Lake Trail," Valhalla said, after we had cleared Pieper Pass.

"How can you tell?" I asked.

"It has to be," was his answer. We were playing for keeps.

Down we went towards a frozen alpine lake on a slippery slope. The next several miles were essentially an obstacle course

*Where to go? Countless are the times that the PCT hiker
is left with nothing but footprints to follow.*

through the snow-filled evergreen trees. A deep arctic-like hush prevailed, broken only by our heavy footsteps. It was Christmas-card beautiful—enough to stir the emotions of even the most hard-bit soul. Some of the time we seemed to be on a trail; other times we were bushwhacking. Most of the time we were on our feet, but not always. Valhalla seemed embarrassed he was falling as much as the tall southerner hiking behind him. Perhaps that was his Nordic ego acting up!

As we trekked further down, the snow lightened up. By late afternoon, we had arrived at Highway 2 in high spirits. Better—or worse—yet, Pretty Boy Joe and Giggles were standing there unsuccessfully trying to hitch. An intrepid middle-aged lady finally stopped to pick all of us up. Unfortunately, we didn't build up a reservoir of goodwill for our future hiking brethren. When we exited the lady's car, I looked in the backseat where the obvious remnants of a hiker's muddy slide stained the backseat of her car.

Chapter 41

Northwestern Hospitality

Eastern Washington Bumper Sticker:

HUG A LOGGER. YOU WILL NEVER GO BACK TO TREES.

Y̶ou couldn't imagine two more different places than eastern and western Washington State. Latte-drinking, vegetarianism, environmentalism, and trendy causes were for the secular intellectuals in coastal Seattle. Much further inland here, they were replaced by a more traditional fare of God and guns. And mountains, I might add. But not many people.

Into this vacuum in the isolated hamlet of Skykomish steps a doughty lady named Andrea Dinsmore and her cigar-chomping husband, Jerry. Running a hiker hostel this far up the trail was a thankless task. After all, most hikers have dropped out by here. But that only magnified the Dinsmore's role. Theirs was a kind of *northwestern hospitality*.

"You shouldn't try hiking this next section," Jerry Dinsmore flatly told us.

"Why?"

"No tellin' how much snow they've gotten up there on Glacier."

Indeed, there was no telling. It kept dumping day-after-day as we cooled our heels in an enlarged room the Dinsmores had retrofitted for hikers. Our initial joy at having successfully weathered the snowstorm soon turned to sullen anxiety.

"My six-month visa expires October, 12th," Valhalla muttered. "I must skip this next section." That immediately put me in a funk. His map-reading skills would be at an ever greater premium.

"If we get out by Saturday," I ventured, "you could make it to the border on the 12th."

"They might send me to Guantanamo," he corrected me.

I tried several lines of rebuttal, but he always went back, albeit in droll fashion, to the same thing, fear of being put in Guantanomo.

"How about it, Backtrack?" I said. "We're roughly the same speed. You wanna' set out together this next section?"

"I can't commit," he quickly said. "Your tent and sleeping bag are not appropriate for these conditions. It could get me in trouble if just the two of us are out there."

A car pulled up and a surprise foursome entered the hiker quarters. Luna and Waffles, followed by Five Dollar and *Pink (What happened to Hollywood? Has Five Dollar pulled it off!).* They walked around passing out hugs to everyone. *What's going on?*

"It's too late to finish," Waffles said. "We're going up to Manning Park (Canada) and hike out to the PCT monument." More hugs and promises to fill in the missing sections next year, and so forth. I didn't like what I was seeing.

I turned to Giggles. We had had running debates on a range of esoteric subjects along the way

Me--"These damn cell phones—you could never make a movie like *Casablanca* again. Cell phones would be going off at the critical romantic moments."

Giggles--"You're just a Luddite, Skywalker." Me--

"No, I'm an enlightened technophobe!"

Most of these scrimmages had ended in stalemate. But here in this cramped hiker hostel in northern Washington with our backs up against a wall, we came to a meeting of the minds.

"Hey, why don't we go out together, Giggles," I suggested.

"I'm up for it," he said.

"We'd have to agree to stay together just to keep from getting lost," I said.

"Oh yeah. In each other's sight the whole time." This quickened my pulse to be sure. Nonetheless, there was a speculative quality to our conversation.

Then the door opened again. In walked a surprise face. *Bob-Rob*. We all had seen him at several points all along the way, but nobody had really known what to think about him. He clearly preferred solitude. But make no mistake—he was a hiker and of the all-weather variety. Now, though, as he entered the room with all eyes on him, everything about him looked different.

"How's it going?" I asked.

"Not," the soft-spoken Washingtonian answered pithily.

"What's it like out there?"

"Unbelievable," he said, pointing to his waist. "Snow up to here for three days. I had no idea where the trail was half the time." He almost seemed like he was trying to convince himself of what he'd just gone through.

A cursory glance at his equipment and clothes revealed everything was well soaked-through.

"Are you gonna' wait," I ventured, "and go back in in a few days?"

"No," he said unhesitatingly. "I'm done. I'll come back next year."

The whole thing was beginning to have an end-of-the-season feel. But I wasn't from this part of the country and didn't want to feel obligated to come back next year. Walking to Canada in some form held out great allure for me.

The only realistic way to do that at this point was skip this snowed-in section and get to the last trail town of Stehekin. One problem, though. *Stehekin* is a native word meaning, "the way through." It may be the single most isolated community in the entire continental United States. There are only two ways to get there. Hike several days over a snowy mountainous range. But we had all just ruled that option out as impractical. The other route was by ferry.

***

Great consolation awaited our decision. The ferry took us over Lake Chelan, the third deepest lake in the United States (the PCT had already passed by the two deepest lakes). We sailed through an almost absurdly gorgeous scene where glaciers had carved out a steep gorge in the rugged mountains.

I honestly would have given my eyeteeth to be hoofing it over these mountains. However, I was at peace with my decision. Long-distance hiking was something to give my absolutely best effort. But as an amateur, it was not worth risking my life like a mountain climber.

It proved to be a great reunion, as well. CanaDoug, Lil' Buddha, and others had come all the way from Snoqualmie, two trail towns back after a harrowing two days trapped in belly-button deep snow drifts, with no obvious way either forward or backwards.

"If it hadn't been for Rocket Man," Lil' Buddha recounted with a tone of amusement, "CanaDoug and I might have died out there. He made us turn around and go back to Snoqualmie." But then Rocket Man had called it a year. He had driven CanDoug and Lil' Buddha north to catch this ferry.

We finally arrived in the tiny seasonal hamlet of Stehekin, where everybody sat down for a big dinner in the only restaurant. At trail towns along the way, we had been eating on a shoestring in places that ranged from good to bad to awful. This meal, though, was special.

"What's your real name?" Whiskey Jet asked.

"Bill Walker," I responded, which drew silly laughs.

"Yours?" I asked.

"Pete Schlerb," he responded to more strange giggles, including my own.

Everybody went around saying their real names and we all cracked up like schoolkids. Perhaps it showed just what a bubble long-distance hikers live in.

Part of that bubble was an antipathy to resume talk.

"Where have you worked in the past?" I asked Lil' Buddha.

"I worked for a couple of giant corporations," he plaintively said.

"What did you do for 'em?"

"I was a salesman," he said. "In other words I was a liar," he joked.

Attitudes toward careers ranged from indifference to just not giving a damn at all. We judged each other by the way we were on the trail, and in no other way. In this sense, you could even say hiking trails exemplify the concept of community.

***

"Nobody should be alone at this point," Meaghan said at breakfast the next morning.

That was music to my ears. The 90-mile section ahead was almost completely isolated, running through the snowy northern Cascades. Serendipitously, the weather had cleared and the next five days looked good. The extended forecast, however, showed bitter arctic-cold swooping down. But if things went according to plan, five days should be enough to make it safely to Canada, and wrap myself in the warm comforts of civilization for the winter.

What great fun this should be finishing with so many of the same people I had bounced amongst almost the whole way. But then CanaDoug walked in.

"Hey, Minnesota is playing Green Bay on Monday Night Football," he announced jovially. "It's Brett Favre's first game back against the Packers. Let's stay and watch it."

"Yeah, but there's that cold front coming this weekend," I countered. "We'll get caught in it if we don't hike out today." To my dismay, however, one person after another began voicing enthusiasm for CanaDoug's idea.

"Skywalker," Lil' Buddha reasoned (picking up on the bear-related humor of the previous evening's dinner), "if you hike out alone, you'll get eaten by a grizzly." Indeed, for the very first time in my life, I would be hiking in grizzly country. The possibility of an encounter concerned me, to be sure. Heck, even the most seasoned outdoorsmen strive to avoid these creatures of virtually mythical strength and appetites. But I wasn't obsessed by it.

"Rare as a Sasquatch spotting," our waitress had told me the previous evening.

No, my biggest concern far and away was cold weather. From my first days on the Appalachian Trail, cold, wet weather had been my Achilles heel. Now I had a five day window to make a break for the Canadian border before possibly getting blasted again. My thoughts went back to the Kickoff last April. "Be finished before October 1," everyone had stated with unanimity. "Anything after that is borrowed time up there."

No way I was staying back even if I had to hike out alone. But I did try to lobby a few of my colleagues to re-consider.

"I may hike out," Not a Chance said ambivalently.

"Hey, we go about the same speed," I said hopefully. Even she was reluctant, though.

Finally though, she unenthusiastically hoisted her backpack and headed back to the trailhead.

***

Twenty-one year old Not a Chance had a style all her own. For starters, she night-hiked more often than not—usually alone. One night recently, she had been walking along when she saw a pair of shiny eyes no more than twenty feet off the trail peering intently at her.

"First I thought it was a bear," she recounted. "But then I practically shit in my pants. It was a cougar."

"How big was it?"

"That thing was huge," she said. "Much bigger than a dog."

"Do you still night hike?" I wondered.

"I don't plan it," she shrugged. "It just kinda' happens."

"How far are you looking to take it today?" I asked Not a Chance, when we arrived at the trailhead.

She hesitated and then said, "I'm supposed to meet a guy I've been dating at Rainy Pass." This seemed a little odd. She had just decided to hike out today. Shouldn't it be clear or not, if she was meeting a guy at Rainy Pass?

We headed off and predictably hiked late. It seemed to elude us that darkness would quickly swoop down on us in northern Washington in October. But then again, I was hiking with the night-hiker non-pareil, Not A Chance. *These next several days could be interesting.*

It was dark when we came to a turn in the trail. No sign. "What do ya' think?" I asked. "Let's try this way," she said. But after a few feet the trail turned scraggly.

"This is what the trail has usually looked like when I'm lost," I said.

"Well, let's go back and give the other a try," she said in a calm, work-womanlike way. We gave it a try. A cold, incessant drizzle—the hallmark of the Pacific Northwest—began to sock in. Nature was, if anything, patient. These next few days, I needed to demonstrate the same.

When we emerged from the woods onto the highway at Rainy Pass, there was no sign of the PCT going forward.

"Maybe that left we headed down at first was the right trail after all," I ventured.

"We'll figure it out," she said, lolling around looking for a path.

"What's the name of that guy you're meeting?" I asked.

"Why?"

"I'll yell his name."

"Ricardo," she answered hesitantly. Soon the shouts of "Ricardo, Ricardo," in a southern accent reverberated through Rainy Pass in northern Washington on a cold, wet October evening. But to no avail. We started walking straight up Highway 20 in a steady drizzle. Finally, we found the PCT, but not Ricardo, and quickly set up camp near the road.

I awoke early after sleeping in fits and starts. Today, I had my game face on.

"It's gonna' be tough to make big miles with it getting dark so soon," I said into Not a Chance's tent.

"Guess so."

"I'm gonna' get out early," I said. "What are your plans?"

"Oh, we'll just have to see," she said non-chalantly.

My confusion was clearing up. Ricardo—if he did exist—

wasn't to be found anywhere around here. Not a Chance simply didn't want to hike with me. Fair enough. Needless to say, anybody has the right to choose their own hiking partner. And I sure as heck didn't want to make myself a nuisance. "See ya' up the road," I said quietly after getting everything packed up.

"Enjoy your hike," came her voice out of her tent.

Other than a brief encounter with a southbound hiker a couple days from now, it would be the only human voice I would hear the next four days.

Chapter 42

Splendid Isolation

All nature is your congratulations.

Henry David Thoreau

Over a journey this long you could fairly say that one becomes a student of beauty. The stucco beauty of the desert had evoked a certain timelessness. The majestic beauty of the High Sierra has blown away mortals throughout the ages. Now, the rolling evergreen forest and white snow-capped peaks of the Northern Cascades connoted a beauty of rugged bleakness. I had never been this alone in my 49 years. Feeling ran high.

At any given time on the PCT, a thru-hiker is bound to have his or head down in a hangdog position, and the brain in neutral. But not now. My overwhelming mission was to not get lost. Every time I saw the trail veering towards snow and ice—which was more times than I could possibly count—a certain dread set in. A fleet-footed hiker named Blue Eyes was traveling a day ahead of me, and I was to strain to follow his footprints every step of the way.

On the third day, I arrived at Hart's Pass running low on water. Because this was a popular campground, I even held out the faint hope of some kind of trail magic. Heck, even talking to somebody would be nice. But the season was over with, and I didn't see any people or cars when the trail entered the campground. Worse yet, I wandered all over the parking lot and down a hill, but came up empty searching for water.

I stood there taking in the gigantic hush. The lonely wind blowing through the mountain passes was the only sound besides the crunch of my slow footsteps (I may not have been as alone as I had thought, however. A few days later in Canada, a former U.S. Army Ranger, traveling a day ahead of me and carrying a sidearm, informed me he had spotted the footprints of a grizzly bear right here in this parking lot—awful glad I didn't see them!).

I meekly munched on some bagels and cold tuna. But I held back on the peanut butter in order to not exacerbate my thirst. Then, with great uncertainty, I hefted my backpack. I had gone 12 miles for the day, and hoped to make at least 10 more. But I needed water, and the data book didn't show any water for those 10 miles. If nothing else, I would have to start filling my bottles with packed snow off the ground and hope for the best with my stomach.

After a half-mile, I heard the welcome sound of tumbling water. Snowmelt was tumbling over rocks and I was able to stick my water bottles in and get a perfect fill-up. I drank almost two liters of cold water right there on the spot and filled up with three more liters. This was a relief. If absolutely necessary, this water should be able to carry me all the way to Canada.

Normally, hikers look for streams to camp near. But not in grizzly country. Here, you find less attractive places. As the sun fell over the hills, I was starting over an area called Devil's backbone. I spontaneously decided to pitch my tent right there a few feet off the PCT. Per hiker convention, I urinated all around it to mark my territory from other animals and got in for the evening. Like a metronome, mother nature called in the middle of the night. Using a urine jar in order to preserve warmth in the tent was a no-brainer in this type of situation. I had long since gotten over my self-consciousness in executing this. But I damn sure wasn't prepared for what happened next.

Per custom, I unzipped my tent and emptied the contents outside of the vestibule. This always made me feel safer as the night wore on and the urine around my tent built up. After all, what animal wants to get near urine. I was about to find out.

Immediately, I heard the breaking of branches and heavy steps coming in my direction up a steep hill. All my efforts the last few days at maintaining a positive equilibrium were suddenly in shambles. Instead, I lay there in white-knuckled terror banging my hiking pole against a water bottle. In the fall of 1978, I had read an article in *Sports Illustrated* about a grizzly attack on a man in Colorado. When the bear had entered the man's tent, he had weighed 180 pounds. By the time the bear left the tent, his remains weighed 75 pounds.

As luck would have it, however, a few weeks before in southern Washington I had run into a couple at a campsite and asked them what northern Washington was like.

"It gets so cold and barren up there," the lady had told me, "the deer come running up when you urinate. The minute you unzip your tent, they head straight for you."

"Why?" I had wondered.

"The salt," she had answered.

Thank God, she was right. Two deer came right up to my tent and began lapping away at the salty urine as I lay there in amazement. Other than that, it was an uneventful evening!

***

"Skywalker," a familiar voice called out.

My heart jumped, at the sound of a human voice.

"Five Dollar," I responded. "What the hell?" We had had these spontaneous run-ins all along the way. But this time was different. He was now headed southbound.

"I applied for the entry permit to Canada" he replied unhesitatingly, "but I've got way too many things on my record. So I had to hike out the way I came in."

"You're going all the way back south to Stehekin?" I asked in amazement.

"No, my girlfriend is picking me back up at Hart's Pass."

"Cool," I said. "Who's your girlfriend?"

"Pink."

Pink.

"Hey, congratulations," I high-fived him. "I remember she was at the top of your list. What happened to Hollywood (her prior trail boyfriend)?"

"Well, you know how it goes," he laughed. "All I can say is that the last two weeks have been great (Unlike most trail romances, this one is still going)."

"Where are you going from here?" I asked.

"I met a guy on the trail back on the trail in northern California that offered me a job at his medicinal marijuana farm. He's paying me $100 a day with a free place to live. Heck, I'm in."

We exchanged info on water and campsites in each direction.

I'm old-fashioned in one respect; I rarely hug other males. But as we readied to depart for the final time, I felt this sudden urge to embrace, which I initiated. Off we went.

Some people just take longer to figure out. In retrospect, the problem may have been that I just haven't seen many quite like Five Dollar. Maybe that's my loss. He was one of the most authentic and honest individuals I've ever met.

John Kennedy once said of Lyndon Johnson, "It's not so much that he's a liar, as he doesn't know how to tell the truth."

Five Dollar was just the opposite. He didn't seem to know how to even nuance or hedge, much less lie. It wasn't always pretty, to be sure. But he wasn't the type guy to keep you awake at night. Come to think about it, that is a general characteristic of the hiking population.

***

The West had had me off balance from the beginning. There was clearly a harshness and unpredictability that I was simply unfamiliar with (Perhaps I should have read the history of the Westward Exploration a little more carefully). Intermittent negative surprises had set me back from the very outset. At this late stage, I had only one mission—get the ship to port; avoid blunders.

My stomach had sunk when Five Dollar had told me, "There's a steep snowfield you'll hit in a couple miles. Don't try anything fancy."

*The northern Cascades have their own brand of beauty and treachery.
Quite a stirring way to finish, if you beat the snow.*

"You haven't got to worry about that," I had told him. I was moving along fine when the PCT cleared a narrow crest. I looked straight down at a packed field of snow and ice. A gunshot wind dominated the bowl-shaped landscape. *Damn.* This could be the game here.

I rushed back below the ridge line and hit my knees. Quickly, I put on additional layers, gulped down some food and advil, and said a quick ritual prayer for faith. *Where does the trail go?*

"There's a trail off to the left," Five Dollar had told me. "Don't take it. Trust me." I started down to the right.

The first few steps were the most treacherous since the worst parts of the High Sierra. Getting off balance could easily send a person careening down the steep snow banks. But there was no alternative, so I dug my legs in as deeply as possible, hewing close to the ground. Gales of wind blasted me. Twenty minutes later I was at the bottom of the snow bowl, and felt like I might have just cleared a major hurdle.

Another complication immediately presented itself. I had been following Blue Eyes' footprints intently the last few days, and knew the size and shape of them by heart. However, when the trail came to an unmarked fork, his footprints appeared to go to the right. But that led to a narrow ledge which couldn't possibly be the PCT (I would later learn that Blue Eyes, who was a truly brilliant outdoorsman, had decided to traverse this ledge as one last challenge). I anxiously studied this fork for several minutes looking for footprints. Finally, I very tentatively decided to go left, and was soon ascending up another snowy mountain pass. The only footprints in the snow were going southbound—presumably those of Five Dollar. These would have to guide me through these nether regions.

***

When I look back on my two long hikes on the AT and then the PCT, one of the things most strongly engraved in my mind is the all-out efforts late in the day. For a person to do big miles, these late pushes were absolutely necessary. I cherish the memory of digging deep to make these twilight surges. This was the last climb on the PCT, and looked like one of the most important of all. If I could just get to the top, it would be all downhill to the Canadian border.

The trail kept winding and winding through the snow. I fervently hoped no more surprises lay ahead—unmarked forks, footprints giving out, steep snow fields, whatever. The PCT serpentined all over the place. I had long since given up trying to predict where it would go. Finally, however, it appeared the trail was going down. Soon I spotted the welcome sight of the lake mentioned in the guidebook and the trail zigged and zagged in that direction. *Home free.* A few miles later at dark I found a flat spot right in the middle of the PCT, just three miles from the Canadian border.

The walk down to the Canadian border the next morning was dominated by an ice-cold wind. I tried all manners of wrapping clothing around my fingers to get them functional; but none were successful. The frost felt like it extended almost up to my elbows. I could take pride in one thing, though. I had definitely made the right decision 90 miles back at Stehekin to hike out ahead of the big group, which had spent the last few days following my size

15 shoe prints. Tonight the temperature was going down to 11 degrees with a chill factor well below zero.

Suddenly, I turned a corner and there was the PCT monument, which any PCT hiker could recognize in an instant. In trail town after trail town along the way, there had been photos of hikers celebrating at this monument, with the narrow swath of tree cuts separating the two borders in the background. The first few trail towns I had gazed at these photographs enviously. But then I had disciplined myself to quit looking at them. I honestly hadn't known if I would ever make it this far.

I had probably worked harder to get here than for anything else in my life. Yet, it ended up not being very memorable at all. Apparently there was a trail register in some compartment of the monument. But even if I had been aware of it, I probably wouldn't have been able to sign it. The motor skills of my fingers were virtually non-existent at this point. The main thing I was worried about was the eight miles to get to civilization at Manning Park. So instead of the customary border celebration, replete with hugs, kisses, merriment, etc., I took the standard five-minute break to gird for the 1,200 foot climb that lay immediately ahead.

That probably says as much about me as a hiker as anything else. It wasn't pretty . . . but I got there.

Epilogue

Those who dream by day are cognizant of things which escape those who only dream at night.

Edgar Allen Poe

I distinctly remember descending Mount Katahdin after finishing the Appalachian Trail and thinking, "This trail is a perfect match for me."

Now as I loped north from the Canadian border on October 9, 2009, towards civilization at Manning Park, my train of thought was different. I had never developed the level of comfort with the PCT that I had with the Appalachian Trail. My inadequacies in matters ranging from gear to maps to camping skills had frequently stuck out like a sore thumb. So often I had been afflicted with uncertainty about what lay next.

Then there was this stark fact. I had hiked every single step of the 2,175 mile-long Appalachian Trail in 2005. Then I had spent the next few years with one overriding goal—to do the exact same thing on the 2,663 mile-long Pacific Crest Trail. Regrettably, I wasn't able to completely pull it off. Due to my foot injury in the desert, the fires in northern California, and the snowstorm in northern Washington, I had to skip a total of 435 miles. That means I hiked a total of 2,228 miles, which was 53 miles more than I did on the AT. I lost 43 pounds to 33 on the AT. So, it wasn't perfect by any means.

Yet when I'm asked the question, "Which trail did you like better—the AT or the PCT?" my answer is always the same. "It would be like asking a parent to choose between two children. They're very different, but I could never decide between the two." It is an honest answer.

The PCT experience offers the priceless experience of intense immersion in the West. The overwhelming feeling is one of liberation, starting with the wide-open vistas, vast spaces, and majestic scenery. Better yet, the geography seems inculcated in the the western people, from their unhurried cadences and strides, to their healthy appetite for the new.

Another day at "the office". By the way, if you have office envy, there is plenty more office space available!

Rare is the individual whose mind hasn't been captivated by the great explorers of centuries past. Christopher Columbus, Captain Cook, and the Pilgrims all crossed oceans on far-flung peregrinations. Countless others made history in the Great American Westward Expansion. Lewis and Clark, Zebulon Pike, and John Wesley Powell, to name but a few. Not for a second would I rate hiking the PCT in the league with these intrepid souls. That age is long gone, and never to return. But that doesn't mean that a person should lose one's adventurousness or curiosity. Quite the contrary.

Consider for a moment the tragic case of Chris McCandless, the protagonist in Jon Krakauer's, *Into the Wild*. So young, but so earnest and thoughtful, McCandless had headed off on foot across the country after college graduation. Given a literary diet overly rich in the Yukon adventures of Jack London, it was perhaps inevitable he would end up in the Alaskan bush country.

"Nothing is more damaging to the adventurous spirit within a man than a secure future," he wrote. "The very basic core of a man's living spirit is his passion for adventure." Obviously, McCandless took his wanderlust too far, for he ended up trapped in the nether regions and starved to death.

Perhaps the most poignant part of the entire story is that McCandless's instincts were quite sound. In fact, on the way to Alaska, McCandless actually hiked for a while on the PCT. Had he just continued, he might have been able to sate his appetite for adventure right there on this wondrous national scenic trail.

The nation's two great national scenic trails (AT and PCT) may be the closest thing that an average person like myself can ever get to an open-ended journey, like the explorers of yore. Both rate among the few things in my life where I can honestly say I've done my utmost. I'm immensely grateful for the experience.

Yet, I would never try to talk anybody into attempting them. They require all-out effort for an extended period of time, and are inevitably accompanied by a certain amount of peril. Rather, my message is directed to the person who says, "I really would like to try them, but I don't know if I'm capable." That person would then be in the same shoes as I was in 2005, when I had set off so full of hopes and fear on the Appalachian Trail, never having even spent the night outdoors. My strongest exhortations to that person would be to put their game face on and step forward.

I distinctly remember arriving at a campsite alongside a lake on a miserably cold, rainy night in northern Washington. All my usual doubts were flaring up this evening, as I struggled to stay warm. While hurrying to erect my tent, I suddenly heard something emerge from the nearby pond. I jerked around to see the smiling face of a nude male heading dutifully to his nearby tent. His trail name—which could indeed be a metaphor for the entire long-distance hiking experience— was *Crazy, But Good Crazy.*

Suggested Readings

White, Dan, Cactus Eaters: Harper Perennial, 2008.

Ballard, Angela and Duffy, A Blistered Kind of Love, The Mountaineers Books, 2003.

Krakauer, Jon, Into the Wild, Anchor Books, 1996.

Krakauer, Jon, Into Thin Air, Anchor Books, 1998.

McDonnell, Jackie, Pacific Crest Trail Handbook, 2009.

Spearing, George, Dances With Marmots, Lulu Press, 2005.

Blanchard, Dennis, Three Hundred Zeroes, Amazon, 2010.

Schifrin, Schaffer, Winnet, Jenkins, The Pacific Crest Trail,

Wilderness Press, 2003.

Ryback, Eric, The High Adventure of Eric Ryback: Canada to Mexico on Foot, Chronicle Books, 1971

Go, Benedict, PCT Data Book, Wilderness Press, 2009

Acknowledgments

Several people helped turn out this work in a timely fashion. Miles Brandon, who proved to be almost embarrassingly helpful while hiking the trail, also assisted me by letting me use many of his photographs. Thanks again, Miles.

Carl Triplehorn of Alaska, who took over one thousand photographs on the PCT, was nice enough to give me access to some of them.

Dave and Nancy Fernbun, avid beach-walkers in Sarasota, Florida, but equally avid readers, offered several helpful suggestions. Of course, their enthusiasm was partly driven by their western orientation, and virtual refusal to acknowledge the mountains in the East as anything more than blips!

Dennis Blanchard, also of Sarasota, Florida, and author of the entertaining hiking narrative, *Three Hundred Zeroes*, showed the generosity that has made him so popular in the hiking community. Dennis knows a technophobe when he sees one, and helped me get the manuscript format-ready for publication.

Jaime Dunn of Knoxville, Tennessee, and an avid mountaineer herself, proved to be genuinely interested in this work, and showed a keen eye for the arresting detail.

Once again, my mother helped with re-supply, by sending out maps and various articles of equipment to various post-offices along the way. She is another example of someone who has absolutely no background in hiking or wilderness adventures, yet gamely warms to the task when engaged. That says a little something about the virtues of the outdoor life.

About the Author

Bill Walker was born and raised in Macon, Georgia. He was a commodities trader in Chicago and London for 14 years, and later a teacher in Latin America. His first book, *Skywalker–Close Encounteres on the Appalachian Trail* (2008), was a narrative of his 2005 thru-hike of the Appalachian Trail. He has subsequently written a narrative about the wildly popular European spiritual pilgrimage, *The Best Way—El Camino de Santiago* (2012). Mr. Walker, who is 6' 11", is currently working on a book on the subject of height. He lives in Asheville, North Carolina.